Awaken Children
Volume 9

AWAKEN, CHILDREN!

Dialogues With
Sri Mata Amritanandamayi

VOLUME 9

Adaptation & Translation

SWAMI AMRITASWARUPANANDA

Mata Amritanandamayi Center, San Ramon
California, United States

AWAKEN, CHILDREN!
Volume 9

Published by:
Mata Amritanandamayi Center
P.O. Box 613
San Ramon, CA 94583
United States

In India:
www.amritapuri.org
inform@amritapuri.org

In Europe:
www.amma-europe.org

In US:
www.amma.org

This Book is Humbly Offered at the
LOTUS FEET OF HER HOLINESS
SRI MATA AMRITANANDAMAYI
The Resplendent Luminary Immanent
In the Hearts of All Beings

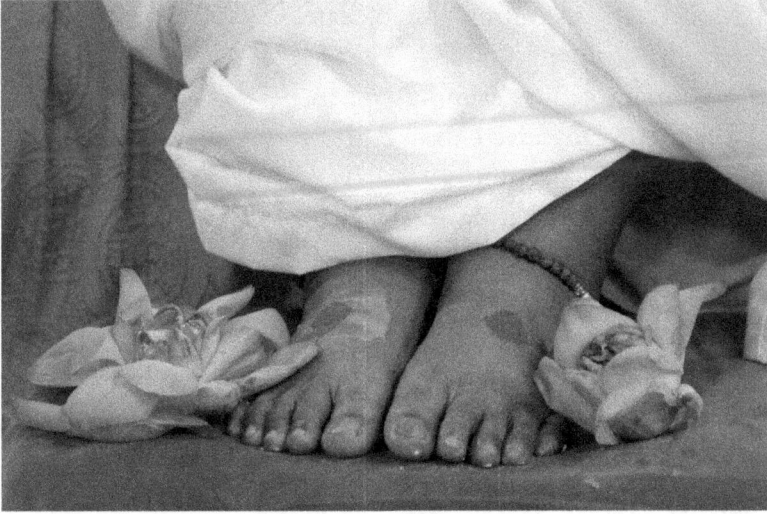

Vandeham saccidānandam bhāvātītam jagatgurum |
Nityam pūrnam nirākāram nirgunam svātmasamsthitam | |
I prostrate to the Universal Teacher, Who is Satchidananda (Pure
Being-Knowledge-Absolute Bliss), Who is beyond all differences,
Who is eternal, all-full, attributeless, formless and ever-centered
in the Self.

Saptasāgaraparyantam tīrthasnānaphalam tu yat |
Gurupādapayōvindōh sahasrāmsena tatphalam | |
Whatever merit is acquired by one, through pilgrimmages and
from bathing in the Sacred Waters extending to the seven seas,
cannot be equal to even one thousandth part of the merit derived
from partaking the water with which the Guru's Feet are washed.

Guru Gita, verses 157, 87

Contents

Author's note

Though Mother's 1987 world tour lasted for three months, I have omitted mentioning many of the details of the tour in this book. I have instead chosen to focus mainly on Mother's dialogues and a few events that I thought would be of most interest to the reader. A more comprehensive version of Mother's tour, including the devotees' and my own experiences, will be published at a later date.

Swami Amritaswarupananda

Introduction

The year 1987 marked a turning point in Mother's mission of spreading Her message of love, compassion, and peace to mankind. The time had come for Mother to go out and gather all Her children, who were waiting for Her all over the world, into Her fold. A few of Mother's American devotees, led by Brahmachari Nealu's brother, Earl Rosner, invited Her to the United States. They had cherished this desire for a long time, and were thrilled with joy when Mother finally accepted. It was decided that She would spend a few days in Singapore, two months in America, and one month in Europe.

One may wonder why Mother travels when She has the power to bless anyone anywhere on the planet, without going anywhere. She simply does it for the benefit of humanity. Just as spring arrives, bringing new life, freshness, and color to the world; and a cool rain brings life to the parched plants and trees after a drought, a true master like Mother arrives in different places, bringing love, hope, and renewal to all of humanity.

Mother sent two of Her children, Br. Nealu and Br. Amritatma Chaitanya,[1] to America, three months in advance, to help prepare the ground for Her tour. An American woman, Gretchen MacGregor, was also going to help with the organization.

Having arrived in the United States, the little group traveled all over the country in an old battered Volkswagen van which had been lent to them by a devotee, and which was clearly on its last

---

[1] A few years later when they received sannyas initiation, Brahmachari Amritatma Chaitanya was given the name, Swami Amritaswarupananda, and Brahmachari Nealu was given the name, Swami Paramatmananda. All of Mother's brahmacharis and brahmacharinis who have received sannyas initiation have the name Puri added at the end of their names (for example, Swami Amritaswarupananda Puri), indicating which of the ten branches of the Order they belong to. Other names of disciples which have changed since 1987 are indicated within parenthesis.

leg. They were eager to let people know about Mother, but, at the same time, it was difficult for them to be without Her for so long. Especially Br. Amritatma suffered greatly from the separation.

Day in and day out they drove across the country, stopping in different cities along the way to give *satsang* (speeches) and to organize Mother's tour. For weeks the old van was their home, in which they slept, cooked, and did their daily spiritual practices. It was a powerful experience, which taught them that Mother is always present, and it helped them to constantly remember Her.

Miraculously, the old van ran smoothly all the way from California to Wisconsin, without the slightest mishap. But on the very day they arrived in Madison, which they had originally decided was to be the van's final destination, it finally broke down, right outside the house where they were going to stay! What else but Mother's grace had brought Her children all the way there?

As they continued to travel throughout the States, they constantly experienced Mother's love and protection, sometimes in the most remarkable ways. They felt Her guiding Hand at every step that She was taking care of everything behind the scenes. Everything they needed for the tour—volunteers to help with the work, financial assistance, suitable halls where Mother could give darshan, etc.—somehow appeared at the last moment.

It should be mentioned here that the brahmacharis were amazed at and deeply touched by the tremendous enthusiasm and kindness of a few individuals, most of whom had not yet met Mother, but were longing to see Her—people like Steve and Kathy Schmidt, Earl and Judy Rosner, David and Barbara Lawrence, Michael and Mary Price, Steve and Marilyn Fleisher, Dennis and Bhakti Guest, Phyllis Castle, George Brunswig, Susan Cappadocia (Rajita), and Ron Gottsegen. Their generosity helped to make the tour possible.

As they traveled, they met hundreds of people along the way, many of whom were so deeply moved by just hearing about Mother, seeing a picture of Her, or listening to recordings of Her singing bhajans, that they knew they belonged to Mother without even having met Her. Some people even had dreams and visions of Mother before they ever heard of Her.

Mother had begun calling Her flock of Western children.

On May 15, 1987, Mother left Vallickavu. The whole ashram was plunged into a state of despair. The scene was reminiscent of when Krishna left Vrindavan 5000 years ago. Mother's brahmacharis and brahmacharinis were so deeply attached to Her that at the airport, where they had come to see Her off, some of them collapsed as She walked into the building.[2] Br. Pai (Swami Amritamayananda), who had to stay behind and look after the ashram, burst into tears. His grief was so unbearable that he fainted.

Just before Mother walked into the building, She touched Her folded hands to Her forehead and bowed to Her children. As everyone responded by bowing back to Her, She said: "My children, Amma needs all your blessings and prayers for the success of this tour. It is for the benefit of all the crying souls out there that Amma is traveling like this. Those who live in other countries are also Amma's children. Amma can hear their prayers and their yearning. It is to soothe their pain, to alleviate their sorrow, and to show them the eternal light that Amma goes abroad. How can Amma not respond when Her children are calling Her from deep within their hearts? Amma will come back to you soon. But in reality, She is not going anywhere. Children, remember that Amma is always with you. Love one another, serve others selflessly, and don't ever forget to do your spiritual practices."

---

[2] At the airports in Kerala, only passengers are allowed to enter the airport building

Mother sought their prayers and blessings only because She wanted to set an example of humility. The *Bhagavad Gita* says, "Whatever is adhered to by great people will be followed by the common masses." Why, otherwise, would Mother ask for such a thing when She Herself has the power to bless all of creation?

When Mother had finished speaking, She stood quietly for a moment. With infinite tenderness, She let Her gaze wander, resting briefly on each of Her children, and then She turned and walked away. As Mother disappeared through the glass doors, everyone called out, "Amma! Amma!" Some of the brahmacharis and brahmacharinis rushed madly towards the doors crying out Her name.

When Br. Amritatma was later told about this, he said: "This proves that Krishna and the gopis really existed. The love of the gopis for Krishna is not a fairy tale, but a true story. Mother is Krishna who has stolen our hearts and made us all mad with love for Her."

On May 18, 1987, Mother arrived in the United States, where She visited the following places: the Bay Area, Santa Rosa, Santa Cruz (May 18-26), Carmel (May 27), Seattle (May 28-June 1), Berkeley (June 2), Garberville (June 3), Mt. Shasta (June 4-7), Santa Fe and Taos (June 8-14), Boulder (June 15-18), Taos (June 19-21), Chicago and Madison (June 22-29), Charleston (July 1), Pittsburgh (July 2), Cambridge and Boston (July 4-9), New York City and Stamford (July 10-14).

On July 15, Mother arrived in Paris and Her European tour began. In Europe Mother visited the following places: Dourdon and Paris, France (July 16-18), Zurich, Switzerland (July 19-21), Schweibenalp, Switzerland (July 21-31), Graz and St. Polten, Austria (August 1-12).

Through this book, the ninth volume of *Awaken, Children!*, Mother's call to Her children continues. And it will continue until we respond from deep within. The response must come because Mother's words are not mere words, but the expression of Supreme Love, the call of the absolute Truth. That call will therefore sooner or later touch and awaken the innocent, slumbering child within us. Mother, the Supreme Master, will then slowly lead us to *moksha*, the ultimate goal of life—a state of liberation from all bondage; from all pain and suffering—a state of infinite joy, bliss, and fulfillment.

Swami Amritaswarupananda
Amritapuri
April, 1998

Amma arrives at the Airport of San Francisco in 1987

America

San Francisco

Mother arrives in the United States

Mother was about to arrive. A group of about fifty people had come to receive Her at the San Francisco International Airport. Most of them had never met Mother before. As they waited, eager for their first glimpse of Her, the TV monitors announced that the flight from Singapore had just arrived. It was 3:40 in the afternoon. Everyone's gaze was fixed on the exit doors where the arriving passengers were coming out. In their excitement, those who were waiting were getting increasingly restless as they tried to catch sight of Her through the doors that kept opening and closing. Finally, as the doors opened, they caught a glimpse of Mother standing next to Brahmacharini Gayatri. "There She is!" everyone shouted at the same time. Br. Amritatma also saw Mother. His eyes were filled with tears. He tried his best to control himself, but the more he tried, the more he failed.

At last, after a long wait, Mother came out into the welcoming lobby with a beaming smile on Her face, and with Her palms joined together in greeting. A devotee garlanded Mother and, as Mother approached, everyone prostrated spontaneously before Her. At the mere sight of Her, many people broke into tears; but at the same time, their faces were lit up with joyous smiles. They could sense Mother's infinite compassion by just looking at Her. As Mother walked past Amritatma, She smiled at him, giving him a look so loving and so intense that it penetrated his soul, filling him with joy and peace.

Amritatma was extremely glad to see his spiritual brothers. With great warmth, they embraced each other, exchanging a few words of love and concern. He also greeted his spiritual sisters, Gayatri (Swamini Amritaprana) and Saumya (Swamini Krishnamritaprana), and inquired about their well-being.

Apart from Gayatri, Saumya, and the brahmacharis, there were three other devotees traveling with Mother: Mr. Gangadharan Vaidyar, an ayurvedic doctor, his wife, and Mr. Chandradas who hailed from northern Kerala. They felt very fortunate to be able to accompany Mother on Her first world tour.

After a short reunion and some light conversation with everyone, Amritatma joined Mother, who was being led by the devotees to a van which was waiting outside. But before Mother reached the door, She suddenly turned right, went up to a chair, and sat down.

Airport darshan

As Mother sat down, She looked at all the people who had come to meet Her and were now gathering around Her. She smiled at them with great affection, stretched out Her arms towards them, and said in English, "Come, my children!"

Amritatma thought, "O my God! Is She going to give darshan to everyone?" He bent down and whispered to Mother, "Amma, we're still at the airport! Isn't it enough if you give darshan tomorrow at the house?"

Seeing the worried look on his face, Mother smiled reassuringly and said, "No. What's the problem with here and now?"

"But Amma," he protested, "this is an airport! The airport officials are watching us. They may wonder what strange things we are doing." But there was already someone kneeling in front of Mother, being enfolded by Her warm, motherly embrace. Mother had started giving darshan. That is simply what Mother is like. How could She, who is the Mother of all, do otherwise?

One after the other, they all went up to Mother and were embraced by Her, and then they sat down on the floor around Her, gazing at this phenomenal wonder before them. They seemed filled with the peace and love that Mother so clearly radiated.

Seeing this unusual event taking place in the middle of the airport, a few policemen and some others came up and watched the scene for a few minutes.

Nowadays, such scenes occur at every airport in the cities where Mother gives darshan. In 1987, when Mother first arrived in America, there was only a small group of people waiting to receive Her. But now, when this book is being written, whenever Mother arrives and departs at any airport in the world, a large crowd is there to see Her.

Many interesting incidents take place at the airports when Mother is traveling. While boarding and getting off the plane, or while waiting in the passenger lounge, Mother receives Her children with open arms, expressing Her love by hugging and kissing them.

About Her hugs and kisses, Mother says: "Amma's hugs and kisses should not be considered ordinary. When Amma embraces or kisses someone, a process of purification and inner healing takes place. Amma is transmitting a part of Her pure vital energy into Her children. It also allows them to experience true, unconditional love. When Amma holds someone it can help to awaken the dormant spiritual energy within them, which will eventually take them to the ultimate goal of Self-realization."

It has happened many times that Mother has grabbed hold of a pilot, air-hostess, air-steward, or passenger who happened to pass by, and has expressed Her all-embracing love by giving them a hug and a kiss. Surprising as it may seem, when this happens the person never protests or shows any negative reaction. On the contrary, without exception, they spontaneously open up to Mother's love. Usually, Mother has taken hold of them and embraced them before they even know what has happened. The receptivity of the strangers, who unexpectedly receive Mother's darshan in this way, reminds one of Her saying, "True love cannot be rejected. You can only receive it with an open heart. When a child smiles, whether it is the child of your friend or foe, you cannot help but smile back because the child's love is so pure and innocent. Pure love is like a beautiful flower with an irresistible fragrance."

In July 1995, when Mother was proceeding to Europe after the American leg of Her tour, an amusing incident occurred. Before going through the passport control, Mother, as usual, sat down on a chair ready to receive the hundreds of devotees who had come to see Her off. Mother was completely surrounded by Her children, who all sat down on the floor around Her, wanting to be as close to Her as possible. Some of the passengers moved away from their seats when they saw the crowd gathering around Mother. An elderly gentleman, who was sitting on a chair, absorbed in a newspaper, wasn't fast enough to move. Before he realized what was happening, Mother was sitting on the chair next to him, and the devotees were swarming around Her, not leaving an inch of space for him to stand up and move.

The poor man looked alarmed and bewildered. What was he to do? He had no choice but to stay where he was and continue to read his newspaper. He buried his face in the paper and tried to cover his head as much as he could with the large open sheets. But for how long could he keep this up? Mother was now giving darshan to everyone. With heavy hearts, and with their eyes filled with the tears of impending separation, the devotees began to sing:

Take me away
Won't You carry me

Let me rest in Your arms for a while
Take me away
Won't You carry me
Let me bathe in the sweetness of Your smile
Mother, take me away
Take me away

Now, the poor old man grew even more restless. Despite people's tears, there was intermittent laughter as Mother joked with someone or played with a child. The man sat as if imprisoned. But, try as he may, he simply couldn't continue to ignore the great celebration of love that was taking place next to him. Every now and then his curiosity gave way, and he would discretely peep out from behind his newspaper. Mother's irresistible attraction had begun to work on him.

To begin with, he glanced at Mother every thirty seconds or so. But gradually, the intervals were reduced to just a few seconds. Finally, he was so captured by the sight that he threw his paper aside and stared at Mother. A few moments later, to everyone's amusement, he asked Mother, "Can I also have a hug? It looks so wonderful and soothing!" Before Mother had time to respond, he fell on Mother's shoulder and was seen in the fold of Her affectionate embrace. Everyone laughed so much at this that all the passengers who were waiting nearby turned around and stared at them.

For a few moments during this incident, Mother's children managed to forget that She was about to leave, and that they would have to wait a whole year for Her return.

A memorable first evening

From the airport, Mother was driven to the Rosners' house. Nealu, Amritatma, and Gayatri traveled with Her in the van.

Mother gave them a brief description of the events that had taken place at the ashram in Vallickavu after their departure. She told them how terribly sad the ashramites and devotees felt about Her leaving for such a long time.

Mother turned to Amritatma and said, "Did you go crazy thinking about Amma? Son, Amma knows your heart so well! When you left India, Amma told Gayatri how hard it would be for you to be physically away from Amma."

Amritatma looked at Mother's face, which showed deep concern and compassion, and said, "Amma, that madness is only occasional. Only if you give that madness fully will I feel truly blessed."

"Son, that is what you asked for when you first met Amma." (Mother was reminding him of the first time he met Her, in July 1979. She had told him then that She was just a crazy girl, to which he had replied, "Amma, I, too, want a little of that craziness.")

Mother now turned to Nealu and said. "How is everything, old man? How is your health?" (Mother sometimes calls responsible people, "old man.")

Nealu smiled and said, "Everything is going well by Amma's grace." He then gave a short account of their visit to different cities and the programs they had held there.

It took them an hour to reach Earl's home. When they arrived, Mother was given a warm welcome. The house was filled with devotees who were all very excited. As Mother stepped out of the van and walked towards the door, everyone was chanting the mantra, "Om Amriteswaryai Namah." Earl and Judy did *pada puja* to Mother's sacred feet, and their two-year-old son, Gabriel, managed to garland Mother. He had been talking with great excitement about garlanding Mother ever since Earl had entrusted him with that task. Whenever he met someone, he would say, "Do you know what? I am going to garland Ammachi!"

After the reception, Br. Nealu insisted that Mother should get some rest after Her long, tiresome flight from Singapore. Without even responding to his request, Mother sat down on a chair which had been lovingly prepared for Her with a beautiful silk cloth.

Before leaving for the airport, Nealu had removed the chair from the living room, because he feared that if She saw it, Mother would immediately sit down and call everyone for darshan. But someone had put the chair back before Mother arrived. Nealu was upset about this because, to him, there was nothing more important than Mother's health, and he desperately wanted Her to get some rest. But it was not to be, for Mother's infinite compassion never stops flowing towards Her children.

Mother now began calling one person at a time for darshan. As each person came up to Her and knelt before Her, She made them rest their head on Her lap, and then on Her shoulder, as She held them close to Her. As they got up and returned to their seats, they looked calm and blissful. Having gone up to Mother for darshan, Steve Fleisher staggered away from Her as if he were drunk. He came up to Amritatma and tried to express what he felt, but he couldn't say anything because, as was obvious by his glowing face, his heart was full to overflowing. Amritatma suggested that he sit down and meditate for a while. Steve went and sat in a corner of the room with a serene expression on his face.

As Mother continued to embrace Her children, She sang two songs called *Durge* and *Radhe Govinda Bhajo.*

> *Victory to Mother Durga!*
> *O Mother*
> *Ocean of Compassion*
> *Mother Kali*

Adorned with a garland of human skulls[1]
Upholder of the world
Victory to the Divine Mother of the Universe!

❧❧

O Radha
Beloved of Krishna
Radha, who worships the Lord of the cows
O Radha, Beautiful One
Who relieves our distress
Beloved of Krishna, the Lord of the cows
O Radha
Beloved of Krishna, the Lord of the cows

When everyone had received Mother's darshan, Mother asked for some fruit. She cut the fruit into small pieces and fed everyone a piece of the prasad with Her own hands. Mother then sat down on the floor and played with Gabriel. After a while She called a devotee who had just arrived. As She embraced him and his head was resting on Her shoulder, Gabriel, who was standing behind the man, started pulling at his shirt saying, "No! She's *my* Mother!" When Amritatma translated this to Mother, She turned to Gabriel and asked, "Is Amma only yours?"

Gabriel nodded his head firmly and said, "Yes!" Everyone laughed at his innocent remark.

Earl and Judy had two sons, Arlo and Gabriel. Both of them were very excited about meeting Mother, especially Gabriel, who was the youngest. Though he was only two, Gabriel was like a twenty-five-year old within a two-year-old boy. He was a very sweet and clever child.

---

[1] The skulls worn by Kali symbolize the death of the ego.

Gabriel had been born to Earl and Judy through Mother's grace. After the birth of their first son, the couple had longed for another child, but Judy wasn't able to conceive again. Earl wrote to his brother Nealu about their wish to have another child. Nealu wrote back saying, "I told Mother that you would like to have another child. Mother said She doesn't think it's in the cards, but She will nevertheless make a sankalpa (resolve) that you will have another baby." Shortly thereafter, Judy became pregnant with Gabriel.

Mother went into the kitchen. She called everyone and then She Herself began serving them their dinner. It was now 11:30 in the evening. Those who had traveled with Mother were exhausted. But even after a sixteen hour plane journey, Mother was still fresh and full of energy. She was spending time with everyone, giving of Herself, offering them Her whole being.

Nealu was walking around feeling restless because he was so worried about Mother. He kept grumbling, "Can't someone make Her go and rest?" But his words had no effect.

A man came up to Amritatma and asked, "Is Mother always like this, or only on special occasions?"

Amritatma replied, "My brother, Her whole life is like this! She simply cannot be otherwise. Day and night, She makes Herself available to everyone who comes to Her. Mother's life is an offering to the world. Wherever She is, there is a celebration—a celebration of pure, innocent love."

The man turned towards Mother, who was still serving food, and looked at Her with an expression of awe and wonder.

At 12:30 a.m., Mother finally retired to Her room.

The first formal darshan in America

Everyone got up early the next morning. Mother's darshan was scheduled to begin at 9:30. During the first world tour, most of the morning programs were held in the homes of Mother's devotees, while almost all the evening programs took place in different halls and churches, except the Devi Bhavas which took place in the living rooms of devotees.

The brahmacharis and a few of the others were now hastily making all the last minute preparations for the morning darshan. People began arriving at 8:30, and by 9, the Rosners' living room was almost full. Mother entered the room at exactly 9:30. As She entered, everyone stood up as a sign of respect. Mother got down on Her knees, bowed down in front of everyone, touching Her forehead to the ground, and then She sat on a small carpet which had been specially laid out for Her. She closed Her eyes and began to meditate, diving deep into Her own world of transcendent aloneness.

The people followed Mother's example and also began to meditate. Mother's presence helped everyone to experience a state of spontaneous absorption. A little while later, Mother got up, seated Herself on the darshan chair, and began giving darshan.

There was no darshan queue in those days. People sat around Mother and waited as She called everyone individually. Mother spent a long time with each person, asking many questions about their lives. Though Mother already knew everything about them, She asked these questions to help them open up. The personal attention people received from Mother, and Her unique way of giving darshan to every individual, no matter how long She had to sit, was an entirely new experience for everyone. It was an experience that filled them with profound spiritual bliss. The healing that happened in Mother's presence was also remarkable.

In those days, when someone asked a question, if the question wasn't too personal, Mother would ask Amritatma to translate aloud so that everyone could hear, and then She would answer the question in such a way that it applied to everyone.

During the course of the day, Mother also sang several bhajans. Now and then, She would enter into a state of samadhi in the middle of a song. When this happened, Br. Amritatma took over and continued the song.

People were so moved by Mother's presence that some of them sang and danced out of pure joy. Throughout the darshan, people sang spiritual songs in English, Malayalam, and Sanskrit, creating an interesting blend of East and West. A man named David played the harp and sang traditional English hymns. The songs, which were sung in the form of prayers, were pregnant with meaning.

> *Listen, listen, listen*
> *To my heart song*
> *I will never forsake You*
> *I will never forget You*

Many people wept as they came up to Mother and were enfolded in Her arms. Radiant with love, Mother's expression often shifted from joy to one of empathy and deep concern as She wiped the tears of those who were crying, consoled and counseled them, and healed their deep inner wounds which had been caused by the past.

A woman from Taos sang:

> *What wondrous love is this*
> *For my soul, for my soul?*
> *What wondrous love is this*
> *For my soul?*
> *What wondrous love is this*
> *To cause the Mother of Bliss*
> *To be born upon this earth*
> *For my soul, for my soul*
> *To be born upon this earth for my soul?*

I will bow before Thy feet
Before Thy feet I will bow
I will bow before Thy feet, Thy feet
I will bow before Thy feet
You who've made my love complete
You who've made my life complete with Your love
With Your love
You've made my life complete with Your love

To the beloved form of Thee, I will sing
I will sing
To the beloved form of Thee, I will sing
To the beloved form of Thee, Amritanandamayi
To Mata Amritanandamayi, I will sing
I will sing
To Mata Amritanandamayi, I will sing

And when from death I'm free
I'll sing on, I'll sing on
And when from death I'm free, I'll sing on
And when from death I'm free
I'll sing and joyful be
Throughout eternity I will sing
I will sing
To Mata Amritanandamayi, I will sing

Someone asked a question: "Amma, how does it feel for you to be here in the West, compared to being in India? There's a big difference, isn't there?"

Mother smiled and replied: "The barrier created by the body and mind is the cause of all diversity. When you transcend that barrier, all differences disappear. Amma doesn't feel there is any difference. All beings are Her children, and all the three worlds are Her dwelling place. That is Amma's experience. Whether it be here or in India, Amma alone is—seeing everyone as Her own Self. If you are one with the Supreme Consciousness, how can there be any sense of difference? For Amma, there is no here or there; wherever She goes, Amma is simultaneously here and there. There is no question of east or west. Though a flower is composed of many petals, it is one flower. The human body consists of many parts, and yet it is one body. In the same way, the world consists of many different countries, cultures, languages, races, and people; but for Amma there is just the whole—there is only One.

"As long as you are identified with the body, there will be division. Body-consciousness makes you aware of time and space; and with time and space, differences arise, such as religion, caste, race, and nationality. That division makes everything appear to be different and separate from you.

"The one Consciousness, which holds everything in creation together, has been forgotten. Because of this, people experience themselves as outsiders. An ordinary person is aware of nothing but differences everywhere. But for the soul who has realized the Self, and has transcended the body, there are no differences whatsoever. For such a soul, everything is part of the one universal Consciousness. He clearly perceives that everything is interconnected; that there are no separate entities, but that everything forms a part of the Whole. In that state you experience yourself everywhere and in everything—here and there, above and below, in all directions, and in the ugly as well as the beautiful. Wherever such a soul goes, he finds his own Self already there. He is always present, never absent; always conscious, never unaware; functioning spontaneously from deep within. He is not a stranger to anyone, because he is the all-pervading Consciousness. In that state, there is not a moment when you are not perfectly aware."

Amritatma, who was sitting next to Mother translating Her words, found himself remembering a day in 1982 when he was preparing for his exams towards a master's degree in philosophy. He was sitting in a room with his professor, who had agreed to come to the ashram to teach him. They were having a discussion about one of the aphorisms of Patanjali's *Yoga Sutra*. The professor didn't believe in Mother. He said to Amritatma, "Look here! I don't believe for a moment that your Mother has reached that state. Of course, I do believe that a state of all-knowing can be achieved through *tapas* (austerities), but I am not in the least convinced that your Mother is omniscient."

Amritatma felt hurt by the professor's remark. At the same time, he took it as a challenge to his own faith. He found himself impulsively saying to the professor: "All right, if that's what you think of Mother, I'll prove to you that She's omniscient. I'll show you how She responds to my prayers. Just give me a moment and see what happens!" Amritatma turned towards the little altar in the room, on which there was a small picture of Mother. He closed his eyes and prayed with great feeling, "Amma, my God and Guru, please don't think I'm being arrogant or self-serving. I myself have no doubts about you, but let the professor understand that you know everything. It would be a blessing for him. But Amma, you know what is best. Let your will be done." Amritatma then prostrated in front of the picture. As he offered his prayer at Mother's feet, he found himself weeping with emotion. Suddenly, he heard someone say, "Mother is calling you!" Amritatma got up on his knees and glanced towards the door. A brahmachari was standing in the doorway repeating, "Mother is calling you!"

Amritatma's happiness knew no bounds. Filled with gratitude, he again bowed down in front of Mother's picture, saying quietly: "Amma, did you respond so quickly to the prayer of this child?" With tears in his eyes, he looked at the professor and asked: "Sir, what do you think now?" The professor didn't say anything as Amritatma excused himself and quickly left the room.

The darshan hut was about fifty yards away. As Amritatma reached the hut, he looked in through the open doorway. The hut was crowded with people seeking Mother's darshan. Mother glanced towards the door, and when She saw Amritatma, She broke into a smile. "Child, did you call Amma?" She asked. At the sound of Mother's sweet, heart-soothing words, an inexpressible joy welled up in Amritatma's heart. He stood there in the doorway shedding tears of bliss. Mother gazed at him intently, and again She said, "Son, did you call Amma?"

Amritatma was so moved that he couldn't answer. Of course Mother knew everything that had happened, so there was no need to tell Her anything. He sat down and sobbed like a child, covering his face with his hands. When Amritatma returned to his room a little later, he told the professor what had happened. In a deeply regretful tone, the professor said, "Who am I to judge Mother? But let me say this—I confess, I do agree with you that Mother must be omniscient."

After this incident the professor became devoted to Mother.

This experience is told here to illustrate the fact that Mother is present everywhere, at all times, because She is one with the Supreme Consciousness. There is never a moment when She isn't everywhere. There is no place where She is absent.

Amritatma also remembered how Bri. Lakshmi once told him about one of her experiences with Mother. This happened before she began serving Mother personally. Lakshmi was working somewhere on the ashram grounds. Due to the heat she felt very thirsty and had an intense craving for ice water. But as the only refrigerator in the whole ashram was in Mother's room, she knew there was no chance of getting any cold water. A few minutes later, a girl approached Lakshmi and handed her a glass of ice water, saying, "Mother gave me this and told me to give it to you."

Lakshmi was astonished and asked the girl to explain what had happened. The girl told her that as usual someone had offered Mother something to drink during darshan. But instead of accepting the water, Mother immediately said, "Give it to Lakshmi. She is very thirsty and wants ice water." Thus the girl brought the glass to Lakshmi.

There are countless such striking examples of Mother's omniscience, which clearly help us to understand that She is not limited by the body or mind, and that Her compassionate heart and helping hands are always there for Her children, wherever they are.

A blissful celebration

A couple, John and Linda, who were sitting next to Mother, said to Amritatma, "The way Mother receives people is beyond comparison. This is unheard of! Her intimacy and the motherly love She gives us in its purest form is exactly what we need. The Western world has never experienced anything like it."

"Neither has the East," Amritatma replied.

John continued, "Look at these people! They're in another world. It is divine healing. Meeting Mother for the first time—Her touch and the way She looked at us—had a tremendous effect on both of us. Mother has taken away so much pain…." Tears welled up in John's eyes as he spoke. His wife, Linda, who was suffering from severe respiratory problems and wasn't healthy enough to travel or even to sit up, nevertheless came to every morning and evening program, just because of the extraordinary peace she experienced in Mother's presence.

As they were talking, an elderly Afro-American man, who had come with his young wife and three-year-old son, suddenly got up and spontaneously started singing and dancing, "We have seen Christ! In Mother, and in Her divine love and compassion, we have seen Christ, the Lord! In Mother, and in Her self-sacrifice, we have seen Jesus Christ, the Savior!" He looked divinely intoxicated, and his joy was so contagious that the rest of the devotees joined in by clapping their hands and responding to the song. The man's little boy was dancing happily next to his father. Within a few minutes, all the devotees got up and were dancing in the Rosners' living room, responding to the lines of the song. The refrain, "In Mother, we have seen Christ, our Lord," echoed throughout the room. The dancing and singing continued for some time until, finally, one by one, everyone sat down and the atmosphere became calm and serene. As they sat down, they spontaneously began to meditate.

That same divine presence of Mother which, a moment ago, had inspired people to sing and dance with joy, now inspired them to dive deep into meditation. Many of the participants had tears of bliss streaming down their faces.

During the first and second world tours, people had the opportunity to spend a lot of time in Mother's physical presence. Sometimes, a person could spend up to ten minutes in Mother's lap, especially when Mother spontaneously burst into song during darshan. Mother would then slip into a state of rapture, and the person who at that moment was receiving darshan could stay in Her lap until the song came to an end. When Mother sang in that state, She rocked from side to side, as if Her lap were a cradle and the song a sacred lullaby being sung to the child in Her lap. This happened only during the first and second world tours. As the number of people increased, Mother stopped singing in this way during darshan.

Because the time allotted to each individual was so long, darshan often lasted from 9:30 in the morning till late in the afternoon—six or seven hours, without Mother moving from Her chair.

Soon after the morning darshan had finished, the evening program would begin at 7 p.m., lasting until the early hours of the morning. Mother consequently had very little time to rest. She simply ignored Her body and its needs for the sake of helping others. One devotee said, "Mother reminds me of the crucified Jesus, who sacrificed His life for the whole world."

Jnana yoga and karma yoga

During a darshan, the following question was asked by a devotee: "Amma, why do the jnanis, those who adhere to jnana yoga (the path of knowledge), usually extol the path of knowledge, while they condemn karma yoga (the path of action)? Even in the Bhagavad Gita, Lord Krishna criticizes the section in the Vedas that deals with karma yoga. He states that *jnana* is the highest. The Lord says:

> *Thus various sacrifices are prescribed by the Vedas. Know all these to be born of action: knowing this you will be free. There is nothing as purifying as knowledge.* [2]

"Amma, doesn't this mean that even Lord Krishna, who was a perfect jnani, was advocating the path of knowledge rather than the path of action?"

Mother: "Son, Amma doesn't believe that the jnanis have claimed any of the differences between the path of action and the path of knowledge that you are implying. Why would Lord Krishna, who set a perfect example of how to live and act in the world, though he was, in fact, *purnam* (complete), and a perfect jnani, condemn the path of action? There is nothing wrong with

---

[2] Srimad Bhagavad Gita, Chapter 4, verses 32 & 38

the words of the jnanis—it is people's interpretations of those words that are mistaken.

"Life can be divided into two aspects: performing actions and enjoying the fruit of one's actions. The body and mind are active during the waking state. In the dream state, the body is inactive but the mind is active, which is why we dream. The impressions that have been created in the subconscious, which is the unfulfilled part of us, are projected as dreams. Also, even if no actions are being done externally, the blood is still circulating and the heart continues to beat; and that, too, is action. In other words, as long as we have a body, mind, and intellect, we cannot refrain from some form of action.

"Although actions tend to be binding because of our attachment to their fruits, an action can also serve as a stepping stone to freedom from action.

Vedic rituals

"There are many rituals prescribed in the *Vedas*. People have a tendency to become too attached to those rituals, rather than understanding their inner significance and thereby transcending them. The Vedic rituals, and the mantras which form a part of them, purify the atmosphere and benefit mankind. Of course they do much good, but they can't be compared to the immeasurable benefit humanity receives from a person who has attained realization. No matter how important and valuable the rituals are, the practitioner should strive to go beyond them and to experience the ultimate Truth within himself. That is the very purpose of religion: to realize that there is no God or Goddess existing separately from our own innermost Self. This supreme experience of oneness with the Truth is the foundation of all religious teachings. What, then, is the point of practicing spirituality or Vedic rituals if it doesn't lead to that oneness? The mere presence, breath, touch, look, and word of a Self-realized soul has the power to purify and uplift those who come into contact with him. Even the wind that caresses his body, and his saliva, has this power.

"It's inadvisable to give too much importance to rituals, and to become too attached to them, forgetting their real purpose, which is to lead the aspirant to the inner experience of the Truth. This is probably what Sri Krishna meant. Amma doesn't claim to know anything about the *Bhagavad Gita*, but She believes this is the reason for the Lord's criticism of the section on the *Karma Kanda* in the *Vedas*. In those days people were probably too attached to the ritualistic aspect of the *Vedas*, while the section on jnana was ignored.

"If Krishna were to be born in this age, He would undoubtedly criticize the so-called jnanis who simply talk about *Vedanta* without experiencing or practicing even a bit of it. He would, however, praise the Vedic rituals. Do you know why? Because we have forgotten those rituals that could be of such great benefit to the world.

"Not only Vedic rituals, but any karma (action) that we do, is meant to help us attain a certain amount of mental purification. But this is only possible if we have the right attitude. Once the mind and the senses have been purified, we are meant to renounce all action and turn inward in search of the Truth. Having attained that purity, the quest to know the truth of existence will intensify and we will automatically turn within. That longing will eventually help us to experience the Supreme Truth. In the state of oneness there are no *Vedas*, and no gods or goddesses other than our own Self. Everything is experienced as one and the same Self.

"The scriptures say that for a person who has attained Supreme Knowledge—the state of *Jivanmukti*, the realization that everything is the Atman—the *Vedas* cease to be the *Vedas*, and the gods cease to be gods.

"The experience of oneness with the inner Truth is the goal of all religions. Why would there be any religions at all if that realization couldn't be attained? Everybody—the people of all nations, from rich to poor, from the illiterate to the highly educated—are of the impression that God is different and separate from them. What is the use of religion or spiritual principles if the so-called teachers and practitioners remain ignorant of the Truth? It is not incorrect to criticize such people as long as they continue to ignore the inner reality. That must have been what Krishna meant by what he said in the *Gita*, for he came to the world with the purpose of awakening people to true knowledge.

"Today the situation is different. People boast of being jnanis without knowing, that is, without directly experiencing, jnana itself. They are of the opinion that a jnani is someone who carries a lot of intellectual concepts in his head. They don't realize that they are simply carrying around a big burden without getting anywhere.

"Karma and jnana are interdependent. You cannot say you are a jnani without first having acquired the necessary mental purification, through the performance of certain actions mentioned in the scriptures (*Vedas*). It isn't possible to simply take a big leap to the state of jnana; it is a question of slow and steady evolution. It is like the development of a child. You can't expect a child to grow up in just a day or two. The child has to go through several stages in order to grow up; it doesn't happen in a moment.

Impatience destroys

"In the same way, spiritual growth is evolutionary, not revolutionary. In their impatience, people tend to be revolutionary. But revolution is always destructive. Unfortunately, in the modern age people demand spiritual upliftment as fast as possible. Instant enlightenment is what they're asking for. Can you imagine a mother saying to her baby, 'I want you to grow up right now! Why do you keep being a child for so long? Hurry up, I don't have time to wait!' What would you say about such a mother, except that she is either extremely foolish or deranged? People expect a miracle to happen. They have no patience to wait or to make any effort. They don't understand that the real miracle consists of the opening up of one's heart into the one Supreme Truth. That inner blossoming, however, is always slow and steady. Everything in nature is evolutionary. God takes great care and is extremely patient, even with the opening of a flower—and the opening of a flower is a miracle. It takes nine months before a child is ready to be born—and that birth is a miracle. God is never in a hurry. He is evolutionary. Real growth will happen only if you're evolutionary.

"Amma isn't saying that supreme realization cannot happen just like that. It could happen at any time, through the grace of the master. But are you prepared for that to happen? There are people who say, 'Why should I prepare for it when I already am that?' Yes, you are that; but what about the burden of negativity you are still carrying? What about your ego? As long as there is any trace of bondage, you have to work on removing that bondage. The feeling that you are the body and mind is a form of bondage; so is anger, hatred, lust, and jealousy. When you're in the grip of such feelings, the Truth that exists within you, which is your real nature, cannot be realized. This is why the process of sadhana (spiritual practices) is needed.

"People have countless wants and demands, which they want to fulfill as soon as possible. They want results but they don't have the patience to work for those results. To become a great artist or scientist, or to make a fortune, people are willing to undergo long-term training, but when the subject is God-realization they demand it instantly. Impatience, however, can only bring negative results.

"Everybody knows the story of the Pandavas and the Kauravas. The Pandavas were born out of *mantra shakti* (the power of certain sacred formulas). When Yudhisthira, the oldest of the five Pandava brothers, was born through the invocation of a deity, Gandhari, who was pregnant at the time, became extremely impatient. She beat her own stomach so hard that she miscarried and gave birth to a lump of flesh. At that moment, a great sage took pity on her and came to her aid. He divided the lump of flesh into a hundred pieces and placed them in a hundred sealed pots. He filled the pots with his life energy and instructed Gandhari not to open them before a certain period of time. But again, Gandhari was so impatient that she couldn't wait, and she opened the pots before she was supposed to. As a result, the Kauravas were born imperfect and evil-minded. They were instrumental in the destruction of the entire clan.

"Because of her impatience, Gandhari couldn't wait for the sankalpa behind the sage's power to take effect. Had she been patient enough, she would have had brilliant, virtuous sons like the Pandavas. But her impatience destroyed the potential goodness and beauty of that part of creation that was the Kauravas. As a result of her impatience, the evil prince, Duryodhana, was born as the eldest of her children. Thus her impatience was the cause of terrible destruction."

Mother stopped talking and sang a bhajan called *Oru Nimisha Menkilum*.

O Man,
While seeking happiness in this world,
Do you experience peace of mind
For even one second?

Without grasping the Truth,
You run after the shadow of Maya.
You will face the same fate as the moth,
Deluded by the sight of a glowing fire.

Having gradually evolved through different incarnations
As insects, birds, and animals,
You have finally been born as a human being.
What could be the purpose of human life
Other than Self-realization?

Cast away your pride and greed,
Leave the life of delusion,
Spend your human life
Glorifying the supreme Brahman.
God-realization is your birthright;
Don't waste this precious life.

When the song came to an end, a devotee asked Mother to elaborate on the story of Gandhari.

Mother: "The human race is heading towards destruction. People don't have the patience to let God's sankalpa work in their lives, or in society as a whole. People are blinded by their impatience and their demands for instant gratification. The ego always wants to take up challenges and fulfill its desires within the shortest possible time. In their hurry, people lose their patience and discrimination, which, in turn, destroys their clarity of vision. If this is allowed to continue, it will end in a disaster. When everyone in society has become blinded in this way, they will clash with each other: individuals will clash with individuals, communities with communities, and nations with nations. Impatience causes disharmony and imperfection. The evils of today's world, which have been caused by people's impatience, are paving the way for terrible destruction. Unless we wake up, it cannot be averted. This is the moral of the story.

"God's divine sankalpa is behind everything in creation. The Divinity is always present, but our impatience closes the doors, preventing God's sankalpa from taking effect in our lives. Duryodhana, the son of impatience, closed all the doors to his heart, so that Lord Krishna's grace and light couldn't enter into his life. Even though he was surrounded by many wise men in his court, none of them were able to open his eyes. Because of his wickedness and extreme impatience, he was quick to jump to conclusions, displeasing everyone around him.

"Only a deep, gradual, steadfast development can have any real effect. God's motto is evolution. Growing into the state of God-consciousness is almost always an evolutionary process. We have to acquire the necessary prerequisite of purity and mental maturity before we can enter into the realm of the Supreme Truth; and that is what we gain through rituals. Once that maturity and purity is attained, we are ready to dive into the ocean of Sat-Chit-Ananda (Being-Consciousness-Bliss), and then there is no more need for action or rituals. While engaged in any action, or while performing rituals, we should keep in mind that Self-knowledge is the ultimate goal. During Krishna's time, people had forgotten the purpose of the rituals they were doing. They were attached to them and didn't make any effort to transcend the ritualistic aspect of religion. They had forgotten that the rituals were meant to lead them to the supreme goal. That is why Krishna criticized them. So, children, don't think that Krishna had anything against the Vedic rituals per se. If you read the *Bhagavad Gita* properly, you will understand what He really meant.

"If you observe a tree, you will notice that the fruit will not appear unless the flowers first blossom and fall from the tree. On the spiritual path, the ultimate fruit is Self-knowledge. To attain that fruit, the flowers of karma (action) first have to blossom and drop away."

In the background, the fingers of David the musician danced gracefully over the strings of his harp as he sang softly:

Soham, soham,
You and I are one;
Amma, Amma, soham,
You and I are one;
Shiva, Shiva, soham,
You and I are one;
Krishna, Krishna, soham,
You and I are one;
Jesus, Jesus, soham,
You and I are one.

The divine touch

The evening program was held at the Quaker Friends meeting hall. A large crowd was waiting for Mother when She arrived. It is remarkable how Mother is able to communicate with people, even though there is no direct conversation.

At the door, Mother was greeted in the traditional way: Her sacred feet were washed, She was garlanded, and burning camphor was waved in front of Her. As Mother walked through the hall, She often touched people as She passed them. She rubbed someone's chest, affectionately ruffled another person's hair, threw a loving glance at someone, patted a cheek, or smiled at someone. All these small gestures had a great impact on those who received them. Having received a touch, glance, or smile from Mother, people often laughed joyfully, while others were so moved that they wept. Mother's glance, for example, was so radiant with love, and Her mere touch could fill a person's whole being with so much joy and peace of mind, that some of those who experienced it went and sat by themselves in a corner and became absorbed in meditation. The faces of others, who looked tense and troubled by the stress and suffering in their lives, were markedly transformed by that moment of contact with Mother.

The program began at 7 p.m. The last song of the bhajans was *Omkara Divya Porule.*

> *Come quickly, My darling children!*
> *You are the essence of Aum;*
> *Remove all sorrows,*
> *Grow to be adorable and merge in Aum.*
>
> *You may stumble My children,*
> *But Mother is walking beside you,*
> *Creating within you*
> *The awareness of Eternity.*
>
> *Darling children,*
> *Always remember in your hearts*
> *That God is Love;*
> *And by meditating on the embodiment of Love,*
> *You yourselves will become that Love...*

Mother replaced the refrain with "Aum."

The song ended with the melodious chanting of "Aum," and the whole audience joined in. The chanting lasted for more than five minutes. It sounded as if Mother was leading the audience into the world of the Supreme Truth, the realm of "Aum," the primordial Sound.

An act of innocent love

At three in the morning, when the darshan was finally over, Mother got up from Her chair and walked slowly out of the hall, lovingly touching everyone who had lined up on either side of Her path. It was cold outside. Amritatma was waiting for Mother beside the car. As he stood there, he witnessed something very moving.

The ground in front of the hall had been excavated for repair work. A broad wooden plank served as a bridge across the hole. The plank was strong, but looked rough and dirty. Though it was cold outside, a devotee called Ken Goldman removed his coat and lovingly spread it over one end of the plank for Mother to walk on. Seeing that it wasn't enough to cover the whole plank, his wife, Judy, immediately removed her coat and placed it next to Ken's. But there was still some space left where the dirty plank showed through. Inspired by their parents, the couple's two sons took off their little coats and carefully placed them over the remaining area.

When Mother came out and saw the four coats lying across the bridge, She said, "Children, what is this? Why are you damaging your good clothes? It's very cold, please take your coats and put them back on. This body was brought up in very difficult, austere circumstances, so Amma can easily adjust to any situation. Amma doesn't need any special treatment." Mother bent down and tried to pick up their coats, but Ken and Judy knelt down in front of Her and said, "No Amma! Please purify our clothes by the touch of your feet, so that when we put our coats back on we will also be purified." As Ken and Judy looked up at Mother, their two children stood close to Mother, leaning against Her. Mother smiled, and with great affection She gathered the whole family in Her arms. And, then, responding to their prayer, She walked over their clothes across the bridge and stepped into the car. The family happily picked up their coats and put them back on.

In the car Mother said, "What those children (The Goldmans) did reminds Amma of what a *grihasthasrami's*[3] family should be like. When my son took off his coat and spread it over the plank, he was prepared to sacrifice his coat and stand freezing in the cold, because he considered it his *dharma* (duty) to protect Amma's feet. When his wife noticed that his coat wasn't large enough to cover the whole plank, she took off her coat as well, feeling that it was her dharma to fulfill what her husband couldn't complete. But her coat wasn't big enough either, so now both the children came forward to complete the work which their parents had begun. Thus the whole family, inspired by an ideal, sincerely supported each other to fulfill a task which they believed to be their dharma. Though a seemingly small incident, each of them sacrificed something for someone else's happiness. It doesn't mean that Amma needed those coats to be placed on the plank, but their example melted Her heart. She felt so much love for those children!

"This attitude should develop, not only towards Amma, but towards everyone. We should lovingly cooperate and support each other for the common good of all, for the upliftment of the entire society. That is our true dharma; and it can take us to the ultimate goal of life, Self-realization. However, it should always begin with the family."

Amazing grace

It was 4 a.m., the following day, and Mother had just finished giving darshan. People had been sitting for hours around Mother,

---

[3] A grihasthasrami is someone who is dedicated to a spiritual life, while leading the life of a householder.

gazing endlessly at Her radiant face, which at every moment seemed absolutely fresh and new to them, and yet so utterly familiar. For hours they had been drinking from the inexhaustible cup of Her divine love, never moving from their seats, except to go up to Her for darshan. Mother finally got up from Her chair, and was about to walk towards the door, when She suddenly paused and stood looking at someone at the back of the hall. She called out, "Mol (My daughter)!"

Everyone turned around to see who Mother was calling. Again, Mother called, "Mol, come!" A moment later, a young woman came rushing up to Mother. With a loud cry she fell at Mother's feet. The woman was sobbing uncontrollably, calling out, "Mother! Mother!" A few people were about to pull her away from Mother, but Mother stopped them saying, "No, it's all right! She's in terrible pain. Let her pour out her grief." So they stood by and quietly watched the scene. A few minutes went by. The woman was still lying prostrate at Mother's feet, weeping profusely. Br. Amritatma and a few others became impatient and stepped forward, asking her to get up. This time Mother didn't say anything, but She stopped them with a stern look.

A few more minutes went by, and then the woman slowly raised herself and knelt in front of Mother. She joined her palms together in a gesture of reverence and looked up at Mother's face. She tried to speak through her tears, but couldn't due to her intense emotions. Mother smiled at her with a look of great compassion and drew the woman close to Her. Again the woman burst into tears. Mother closed Her eyes and seemed to slip into a different world. She caressed the woman, stroking her hair and murmuring softly, "Mol... mol...."

Then, gently, Mother said to her, "Darling daughter. Child, don't cry. Amma knows your heart so well!" At one point those who were present noticed that Mother was wiping the tears from

Her own eyes. When they saw this, many of them were unable to hold back their tears.

This reminds one of Mother's saying: "When you are in Amma's presence, She becomes you. Amma is like a mirror. She simply reflects the inner feelings of Her children."

Eventually, the woman managed to calm down. Mother gave her one more hug, kissed her gently on both cheeks, and then walked slowly out of the hall.

As Mother left the hall, She affectionately touched everyone She passed. Her love permeated the atmosphere. A woman spontaneously began to sing *Amazing Grace*, and everyone joined in. Then, Mother, the very source of all grace, got into the car and was driven away.

The next day, the woman who had wept so profusely at Mother's feet, told Br. Amritatma what had happened to her. She had come to the hall just before the program started, and had sat at the back of the room during the entire program, watching Mother giving darshan. She herself had no intention of going up to Mother, and there was a reason for her resistance. She had made a few serious mistakes in the past, which she thought were unforgivable, and was feeling extremely guilty about it. As she watched Mother, and the limitless love that Mother showered upon everyone, the woman thought that a sinner like herself didn't deserve to receive such love. Having decided not to go for darshan, she sat there crying throughout the program. But Mother saw her and called her at the end, knowing all about her mental agony.

A few days later, on the way to an evening program, Br. Amritatma asked Mother why She had waited that night until the very end to call the woman.

Mother: "By sitting in Amma's presence and watching Amma for such a long time, that daughter suddenly became conscious of the terrible burden of guilt she was carrying, and this awareness created the urge to empty it all out and be free. The deep feeling of Amma's love, which she experienced while sitting there at the back of the hall, helped to relieve her inner pain. All those tears washed away her guilt, and finally, when Amma called her, she was ready to unburden herself and find the peace she longed for. This couldn't have happened if Amma had called her at the beginning of the darshan, because a certain amount of time was needed for her to open up. Everything is meant to happen in a certain way, only then will it have a lasting effect.

"A sinner—but, in fact, there are no sinners; for the state of enlightenment lies hidden in all human beings, even in the worst 'sinner', just waiting for the right moment to emerge. So, no one is really a sinner. There is only the Atman. Amma is using the word 'sinner' only to explain something.

"A sinner can find peace only in the presence of a great master. For in the master's presence the mind is able to flow freely. In that atmosphere of unconditional love, all sins melt away. The closed dam of the mind opens up, allowing the hardened mind and its emotions to soften and flow unhindered.

"That daughter had become trapped in her pain. She had never had the opportunity to rid herself of the guilt and grief which had stagnated in her mind, because there had never been any favorable conditions for this to happen. So the pain had stayed hidden deep within her.

"You try to cover up your pain with different thoughts, objects, and pleasures. For example, you buy a new car or a new house, find a new boy- or girlfriend, and as you continue to cover up your pain with layer upon layer of distractions, the pain hardens with age; it becomes stronger and its hold more subtle. You go to a psychotherapist, but what can he do? He is trapped in his own mind. All he can do is help you to cover up your pain even further, and the pain remains within you, without any possibility of being removed. Whoever tries to help someone remove such pain will find that, unless his own consciousness is at a higher level than that of the person he is trying to help, no real healing or change can take place. What really matters is your level of awareness. A realized soul is at the highest level of consciousness; he has reached the highest peak. In his presence all sorrows are removed and the wounds of the psyche are healed spontaneously.

"Only a satguru (Self-realized master) can bestow the necessary grace and create the right conditions that will uncover your pain. That is exactly what happened here. The woman's pain was unmasked. Amma's presence helped her to unburden herself of the guilt she had been carrying around for so long.

"The best way to get rid of the great burden of guilt, which is like an infected wound gnawing at you from within, is to become fully conscious of it. This can happen only in the presence of a true master. The master shows you the deep wounds that are festering within you. He helps you to become aware of the serious damage those wounds could cause you, how they could destroy your whole life; and eventually, through his infinite love and compassion, those wounds are healed.

"Amma has heard a story that will perhaps help you to understand.

"There was a rich man who was suffering from overwork and severe stress. Because of this he completely lost his peace of mind. He went to different doctors and healers seeking a cure for his dilemma. Everyone, including his friends, urged him to retire from his work and rest, to stay at home and enjoy a peaceful life. But neither their advice nor the medicines he was given seemed to help him. One day he heard about a great saint who lived in a remote cave. He was so desperate that he decided to visit the master. After a long, arduous journey he finally reached the place. Although it was freezing cold, the saint was sitting naked in the cave. He gestured quietly to the visitor to sit down next to him, and then he closed his eyes and went into a state of samadhi. The saint remained in that state for three days, while the visitor continued to sit there patiently in the ice-cold cave, without any food or sleep—so great was his desire to free himself from the pain. On the third day the saint opened his eyes and said to him, 'Retire from your work and rest. Stay at home and enjoy a peaceful life.' The man listened to what the saint had to say and went home.

"A few days later his friends came to see him. They were surprised to see how peaceful and contented he seemed. They wondered how such a transformation could have happened to him in such a short time. When he told them about his visit to the saint, and what he had said to him, they exclaimed, 'But that's exactly what we have been telling you all along!' The man smiled and said, 'Perhaps those were the words you used. But when I heard those same words from a true master, I suddenly saw their real, inner meaning. For when the Master uttered those words, I had a revelation. It dawned on me that to "retire from work and rest," means to withdraw the senses from the world of diversity, and to "stay at home and enjoy a peaceful life," means to dwell within the Self, seeing everything as a manifestation of God. The Master's presence and the power behind his words removed all my fear and tension. At last, I am experiencing real peace of mind.'

"Children, only in the presence of a Self-realized master can any real transformation take place. However, both in that daughter's case and in the case of the man in the story, peace of mind was experienced only after they had made the necessary effort. But, actually, there is no effort to be made as such, because there is no force or strain involved. The effort is effortless and spontaneous—it simply happens: the gates of the heart open up, letting the master's grace flow in, bringing new light and energy into your life."

What Mother said about the woman proved to be true because one day, soon thereafter, she came back to see Mother and told Her that she felt like a different person, that for the first time in years, she was relaxed and at peace with herself.

Amritatma asked Mother another question: "Amma, you could have removed her pain by your mere sankalpa, without her having to cry for such a long time. Why didn't you do this?"

Mother: "Son, that is exactly what happened. Amma's sankalpa was at work—it's always there. What do you think inspired the woman to come and see Amma in the first place? And if she had come of her own accord, she might simply have left, instead of sitting at the back of the hall, crying throughout the entire darshan. What made her sit there for so long? And finally, what was it that made her open up to the extent that she did? Do you think all this could have happened without Amma's sankalpa? Her own effort would not have been enough. There is grace and a divine sankalpa behind everything.

"Situations that cause you to open up and develop inwardly can only happen through God's or the guru's sankalpa. Nothing is accidental. We should be able to see this."

The first Devi Bhava

The first Devi Bhava was held in the living room of Earl's house, in a small temple shrine which had been specially made for the occasion. In the early evening, before the Devi Bhava, Br. Amritatma presented Mother's life story in the traditional katha form, illustrated with songs that were woven into the narration. Everyone was deeply moved by it; especially since most of them had just met Mother and didn't know anything about Her remarkable life.

The house was cram-packed; there were people everywhere in the house, and outside in the garden. After the story telling, people sat in the living room in front of the closed temple waiting for the Devi Bhava to begin. They didn't know what to expect. They had been told that Mother was about to reveal Her oneness with the Divine Mother in a more tangible way.

Mother once said to a few of Her disciples, "If you were to really see Amma as She is, it would overwhelm you—you couldn't possibly bear it. Because of this, Amma always covers Herself with a thick layer of Maya (illusion). But during Devi Bhava, Mother removes one or two of Her veils, revealing a little more of what She really is."

On this night—Mother's first Devi Bhava in the West—it seemed to the brahmacharis that Mother removed even more of Her veils than usual. It turned out to be an unforgettable night for all those who were present.

Suddenly the curtains, which were made of different colored silk saris, opened and the brahmacharis started chanting the Durga Suktam,[4] as they always did at the beginning of each Devi Bhava.

Mother was sitting on a chair, wearing a beautiful deep green silk sari and the traditional crown of Devi, the Divine Mother. People were entranced by what they saw. During the daytime darshan one could clearly see and feel Mother's divinity in a way that no words could describe. But now it was revealed to them in an even more powerful way. Her face was utterly radiant with the power, beauty, and compassion of the Divine Mother. And that radiance spread throughout the room, permeating the atmosphere like a glorious fragrance. Mother was so filled with divine energy that Her whole body visibly vibrated with power,

---

[4] Mahanarayana Upanishad

and this continued throughout the Devi Bhava which lasted until the early hours of the morning.

One by one people went up to Mother and were embraced by Her. When Mother touched them they were given a direct experience of a supernatural power which was very subtle, and yet, immensely powerful. Some people compared it to being charged with a powerful current, which was extremely soothing and uplifting. Some people had the experience of being purified, and their negativity was removed. Others were transported to a transcendental state of awareness beyond time and space. Throughout the night, many people sang and danced with joy. The brahmacharis sat in front of the temple, singing bhajans. At the beginning of the Bhava darshan they sang, *Jaya jaya devi dayamayi ambe.*

> *Victory to Mother, who is full of kindness!*
> *O Mother, please give me the bliss*
> *Of Your ocean-like compassion;*
> *Utter the Vedas to Your servants*
> *O my Goddess, Amritanandamayi.*
>
> *By remembering Your Lotus Face,*
> *Our sins and our fears of becoming are destroyed.*
> *O my Goddess, Amritanandamayi,*
> *Who is attached to Pure Dharma;*
> *Giver of auspiciousness.*
>
> *O Mother,*
> *Who urges us to give up*
> *The comforts of the mortal world;*
> *Creatress of the Universe,*
> *Whose nature is purity itself*
> *O my Goddess Amritanandamayi.*

O Great Holy One,
Worshipped by the devotees;
With a pure enchanting smile on Your face,
You dwell in the supreme state,
untouched by desire
O Amritanandamayi.

You have been born as the Goddess of Wisdom
To rid us of this sorrowful world.
O Amritanandamayi,
May Your holy feet transmit their brilliance
Into our hearts, forever.

You have been born for the sake of the miserable;
Your sacred aim is the well-being of others.
O my Goddess Amritanandamayi,
Who has a human form,
Yet whose real nature is Being-Awareness.

You teach us to discriminate between the Self
and the non-Self,
So that our minds will be purified.
Being immersed in the Atman
Your soft words flow out in a nectarous stream
O Amritanandamayi.

Later that night, at the end of the Devi Bhava, Mother stood up and walked to the front of the shrine, and standing before the people, she showered handfuls of flower petals on everyone, worshipping the Supreme within each person. And then, as She stood before them, turning Her body slightly from side to side, Mother underwent a visible transformation.

It seemed to Br. Amritatma that Mother had suddenly grown larger and that Her face was quite different. Though Her boundless compassion still shone in Her eyes, he no longer saw the sweet, gentle Mother before him, but the immensely powerful, awe-inspiring form of Devi, the Mother of the Universe, in Her more impersonal form. And as Mother revealed this one aspect of the infinite aspects of Her Being, he and the other brahmacharis sang *Om Bhadrakali.*

Aum Bhadrakali,
O Goddess, who gives us refuge,
Enchantress and Mother,
Bless me!
O Goddess, who killed the demon Chamunda,
Please lovingly protect Your people
and make them happy!

We bow to Your Lotus Feet,
Which are adorned with golden anklets.
O Chandika,
Beautiful One,
Great Dancer,
Bless us with Your glance of Grace!

O valiant Bhairavi,
Who has severed the head of the demon Darika;
Seeking refuge at Your feet,
We sing your praises!
Ocean of Grace,
We bow down to You.

Carmel

The all-knowing Mother

In Carmel, Mother held an evening program in the hall of the Women's Club. Mother stayed with Nealu's and Earl's cousin, Ron Gottsegen. Ron, who was in his early fifties, and who owned a highly successful electronics company, felt deeply attracted to Mother from the first moment he saw Her. In the afternoon before the evening program, Mother was sitting by Herself on the vast lawn in Ron's garden, when Amritatma came out and joined Her. As he sat down next to Her, She said, "Ron has the qualities of a true seeker. He will renounce everything one day. He is my son." (This is exactly what happened. Ron was later to buy some land in San Ramon and give it to Mother as an offering of love; and that land was to become Mother's ashram in California. Ron would also later be in charge of organizing the development of Mother's super-specialty hospital in Ernakulam, and go and stay with Mother permanently in India.)

❧❧

Seattle

In Seattle, Mother stayed with Mr. and Mrs. Hoffman. The first evening program was held at their house.

Ever since Mother had arrived in America, She had been writing short letters to each resident at the ashram in Vallickavu, because She knew how much they were suffering from being separated from Her. During whatever little free time She could find between the morning and evening darshans, Mother was writing letters.

One evening Mother said, "The morning meditation has just come to an end at the ashram in India. Amma can see all Her children sitting together in front of the meditation hall. They are thinking about Amma, and they are very sad. Some of them are crying because they miss Her so much!" Mother mentioned the names of those who were crying, and then She closed Her eyes and sat quietly with tears trickling down Her face.

When the darshan was over that evening, Mother expressed a wish to talk to all the ashramites in India. So they telephoned Mahadevan, one of Mother's devotees who lived in Alleppey, a town near the ashram, and arranged that all the ashram residents would be waiting there at the same time the next day.

The following night after the evening program, Mother telephoned Alleppey and spoke to Her children, who had been brought there from the ashram. They were eagerly waiting to hear Her voice over the phone. Mother asked them if they were sad. They told Her that they had been especially sad the day before. They had been sitting outside the meditation hall after the morning meditation, thinking about Mother and crying—and now She was calling them! With words laden with compassion, Mother tried to console them over the phone. She told them that She was always with them and had seen them the day before. When She finally put down the receiver, She told those who were present how sad Her ashram children were; and how it broke Her heart when She heard them calling, "Amma!" over the phone.

It was clear that the intense longing of Her children in India had made Mother respond by telephoning them.

The meaning of Her tears

You may wonder how a great master like Mother could cry. Once, when Br. Srikumar (Swami Purnamritananda) had to be away from Mother, and Mother was reading a letter he had sent Her,

Br. Amritatma noticed that She was weeping. The letter contained a song that Srikumar had written called *Arikilumenkilum.*

The sun has set in the western ocean;
The day has begun its lament.
It is only the play of the Universal Architect,
So why should you, O closing lotuses, feel dejected?

This world, full of misery and sorrow,
Is but the drama of God, the Creator;
And I, the onlooker, am a puppet in His hands
I watch, but have no tears to shed.

Separated from You,
I am burning like a flame;
My mind is burning and burning.

I am being tossed about
In this ocean of grief,
Unable to find the shore.

When Amritatma saw Mother's tears, he thought, "How can Mother, who is beyond all feelings, cry like this?" Later when he asked Mother this question, She replied, "Son, in that letter and in the song that Srimon (my son, Sri) had written, Amma felt his innocent longing very strongly. Amma simply mirrors everything, and the reflection of his innocence made Her cry. When you cry or laugh, the image in the mirror does the same. Likewise, in the state of realization, you easily become the other; but you are not attached because your identification is merely a reflection. You don't become attached to or identified with anything. A real master responds to the calls of his devotees and disciples. But the response depends on the intensity of the disciple's call, it depends on his faith and his love for the master.

"Everyone is part of the universal Consciousness. So when you call out to God from the innermost depth of your heart, the waves of that call will reflect in a great soul who is one with that Consciousness—and there is a response. You may see tears in Amma's eyes, but don't mistake them for tears of sadness. They are simply a response to the innocent call from the other end.

"Sri Rama wept when Sita was carried away by the demon, Ravana. He even asked the birds, animals, trees, and plants if they had seen his beloved Sita. Rama's tears were reflecting the pain Sita felt at being separated from her beloved Lord. Similarly, tears welled up in Sri Krishna's eyes when He met his great devotee Sudama. The tears in Krishna's eyes were mirroring Sudama's devotion towards Him. Even in worldly love we can find such examples—provided the love is genuine. The intense feelings of one lover is reflected in the other.

"The lover calls and the beloved responds; the disciple calls and the master responds; the devotee calls and God responds. But the nature of the response depends on the call.

Distancing yourself from situations

"However, the response is just a reflection, because God is beyond everything. He is the Witness Consciousness, completely untouched and detached. In that ultimate state, when you just witness everything that happens—all the experiences you go through, both good and bad—there is a distance between you and each situation.

"Suppose someone dies, not in your family but in the family of a friend. You go to your friend, you sit with him and try to console him. You say to him, 'Don't be sad, my friend. This is part of life; we all have to die some day. But remember that the soul is eternal—only the body perishes.' You are able to say this because there is a distance between you and the situation.

59

"But if a death occurs in your own family, your attitude will be quite different. You will then suffer because you are too close to the problem.

"A famous surgeon who has done thousands of operations wouldn't want to operate on his own wife or child, because he is too attached to them. If someone in his immediate family needs an operation, no matter how experienced or great a surgeon he may be, he will let another surgeon perform the operation. Likewise, a psychologist is too identified with his own problems to really be able to analyze or counsel himself; so he goes to another psychologist for help. A jivan mukta, on the other hand, simply witnesses everything that happens in and around him. He may express different feelings, but he is not attached to them. He is there—totally present—and yet not there."

Farther than the farthest, nearer than the nearest

During the last morning program in Seattle, the following question was asked by an American devotee who was studying the Indian scriptures:

"The *Upanishads* say that the Paramatman (the Supreme Being) is far away, and at the same time, very near.[5] I'm confused about this statement. How can something be far away and near at the same time? Amma, could you explain this?"

Mother: "Son, that which is everywhere is always near and far away at the same time. The Paramatman is everywhere. We are born within the Supreme Self; we live in it, die in it, and are again reborn within it. It is not a distant entity. The Paramatman is truly 'nearer than the nearest.' The apparent distance is due to our ignorance. As long as there is ignorance, the Self (Atman)

---

[5] Tat dūre tadvantike (That which is far away is very near.)—Ishavasyopanishad (verse 5)

will appear to be far away, to be 'farther than the farthest.'[6] Once the misconception that we are the body is removed, that which is 'farther than the farthest' becomes 'nearer than the nearest.' We realize that we have never been away from the Paramatman, that we have always existed within it—it was always *here*.

"Imagine that you are standing on the seashore watching the horizon. At a particular point in the distance, the horizon appears to be melting into the ocean. It looks as if the sky is meeting the earth. If there is an island out there, it may look as if the trees on the island are touching the sky. We may think that if we go there, we will arrive at the meeting point of earth and sky. But instead of reaching the horizon, we would find that the horizon appears to be still further away. As we move towards the horizon, it continues to recede from us, so that we can never catch up with it. When we were standing on the shore, the horizon seemed to be touching the island and the trees, but as we approached the island, the horizon moved away. Where, then, *is* the horizon? It is right here, where you are. You and the horizon are at exactly the same point. In the same way, the Paramatman is not somewhere far away—it is within you. In truth, you yourself are the Paramatman.

"People often say, 'I am sad.' They are saying that they *are* the sadness. Whenever they feel sad, they become immersed in it. They begin to identify with their sorrow until they feel they are that sorrow.

"The Paramatman, the Supreme Consciousness, is very close. But because of our wrong identification with pain, pleasure, sorrow, anger, and other emotions, which are caused by our wrong understanding that we are the body, rather than consciousness, we experience a distance. This identification is ignorance. Once

---

[6] Dōrāt Sudōre tadihāntike cha (Farther than the farthest, nearer than the nearest.) Mundakopanishad (3:1:7)

you transcend that ignorance and are no longer identified with the body, you will not experience that you are in pain, or that you are the pain—but only that you are aware of the pain. You become a witness, simply watching the pain or whatever sensation it may be. Your consciousness stays detached from what is happening to the body. When this realization takes place, the Paramatman will be nearer than the nearest. But until then, it appears to be farther than the farthest. This explains why that which is far away is also very near.

"There is a story about a woman who had an intense desire to get married. For years she had been trying to find a suitable husband, but she hadn't met the right person. Finally, she gave up. She decided to console herself by traveling around the world. She traveled from country to country, from continent to continent; and then one day when she was staying in a hotel at the other side of the world, she met a wonderful man, and the two of them fell in love. He turned out to be her perfect soul mate. What astonished them both was not only the fact that they came from the same city, but that they actually lived in the same apartment building and that their apartments were right next to each other. They had been next door neighbors for years, without even noticing each other!

"Children, you may search for God everywhere, but you won't find Him because He is closer to you than you could ever imagine. He appears to be far away, only for as long as you remain ignorant. Remove your ignorance, shake off your identification with the body and transcend it, wake up and be aware; then you will realize that God is 'nearer than the nearest.'"

After the program in Seattle, Mother flew back to San Francisco.

Ganesha

In the morning, Mother, the brahmacharis, Gayatri, and Saumya left the Bay Area in a small recreational van, lovingly offered to Mother for Her trip to Mt. Shasta by Dennis and Bhakti Guest. The van wasn't big enough for everyone, but because they had such a strong wish to be with Mother, they all somehow managed to squeeze in. On the way, Mother stopped in Garberville, a small town on the way to Mt. Shasta, where She held a retreat program at a lodge, surrounded by redwoods and immense sequoia trees. Responding to their invitation, Mother also visited Ken and Judy Goldman, who lived in a mobile home not far from Garberville.

The Goldman's two small sons were very drawn to Mother. During Her visit, they followed Her around everywhere. Mother taught them to sing a song. Repeating each line after Mother with great enthusiasm, they sang, *Devi Devi Devi Jagan Mohini.*

> *O Goddess,*
> *Enchantress of the world,*
> *Chandika,*
> *Destroyer of the demons, Chanda and Munda;*
> *O Chamundesvari,*
> *Divine Mother,*
> *Show us the right path across the ocean of transmigration.*

The two boys asked Mother to play with them. Mother couldn't reject their innocent request, and so She spent some time playing with the two children. Later, while sitting with the family, Mother asked the boys, "Will you be as innocent and have the same devotion when you grow up?" The boys immediately shook their heads in affirmation.

Judy Goldman was so deeply moved by Mother's presence that she burst into tears and couldn't stop crying. Ken was very excited, and was eager to show Mother his collection of Ganesha icons. Mother looked at the Ganeshas with great interest. She reached out and lovingly caressed the big belly of one of the statues, and remarked with a laugh, "What a hungry man! He has the whole universe in this belly!"

Mother pointed at the elephant god's round stomach and said, "The big stomach symbolizes the true seeker's unappeasable hunger to know the Truth. Ganesha's big ears represent shraddha, the capacity of a sadhak (aspirant) to 'hear', that is, to imbibe, the subtle spiritual principles. An elephant can uproot a huge tree with its trunk, and it can also pick up a small needle. So Ganesha's trunk signifies the sadhak's ability to grasp both the gross and the subtle principles.

"Ganesha's mouse represents desire. Just as one small mouse can destroy an entire crop, a single desire can destroy all our virtues. But a Self-realized soul (Ganesha) has complete mastery over his mind and his desires. That is why He rides on a mouse. At other times, the mouse sits at the feet of Ganesha, gazing intently at the Lord's face, without touching the sweets that are kept in front of the god. This means that a Self-realized soul is the Lord of his own mind; his mind will only move at his command." Mother suddenly looked at Ken and called him "Ganesha." Ken joyfully accepted his new name.

On the morning of their departure, Mother meditated with the brahmacharis and the others beside the swimming pool at the lodge. At ten o'clock Mother left for Mt. Shasta. This trip turned out to be one of the most memorable events of the whole tour.

Faith is more important than reasoning

On the way, Nealu thought it was a good opportunity to talk to Mother, so he asked Her a question:

"Amma, spiritual science always stresses the importance of functioning more from the heart than from the intellect. In fact, I sometimes feel that intellectual reasoning and knowledge is being put down by some of the spiritual masters. Why do they do this?"

Mother: "Son, spirituality is more a question of faith than a subject for intellectual analysis. True faith will develop when the intellect is put aside. This doesn't mean that intellectual knowledge is irrelevant. The intellect does have its place, but it shouldn't be overestimated. Don't think that spirituality is nothing but scriptural knowledge and intellectual analysis. This is often where the problems arise. It is important to create a balance between the intellect and complete trust in the spiritual principles. Your knowledge and reasoning power may, for example, help convince others about the science of spirituality; it may help satisfy their intellectual thirst. However, for your own spiritual development, faith is much more important than reasoning.

"In your spiritual practices, faith is of far more help to you than the intellect. To be able to meditate, you must have complete faith in what you are doing. While engaged in any type of sadhana, you should put aside all doubts, questions, and pondering and focus completely on your spiritual practices; otherwise, you cannot progress spiritually. If you don't have faith, you should try to develop it by seeking the guidance of a satguru. Intellectual knowledge has its own place; when used in the right way it gives you a certain amount of mental strength and determination. But to become grounded in what you have learned, you need to do rigorous practices. When it comes to actual practice, unconditional faith is what you need. So it's a question of creating a harmonious balance of faith and knowledge.

"To remember God, you have to forget. To be really focused on God is to be fully and absolutely in the present moment, forgetting the past and the future. That alone is real prayer. This sort of forgetfulness will help you to slow down the mind, and will enable you to experience the bliss of meditation. Genuine meditation is the end of all misery. All suffering is caused by the mind, and the past is of the mind. Only by letting go of the past, which can be achieved through meditation, is it possible to become established in the Self or God.

"In fact, we already have this capacity to forget and remember. It is done quite often. For example, when a doctor is at the hospital, he forgets about his home and his family. And when he goes home to his wife and children, he has to forget about the hospital and his persona as a doctor, if he wishes to be a good husband and father. In the same way as the doctor forgets his role as a doctor when he is at home, if we want to remember God and focus on the object of our meditation, we have to forget the past, and we even have to forget ourselves. We all know how to do this, to a limited extent, but we haven't yet learned how to tap into the realm of Supreme Consciousness. To be able to drop one aspect of life and embrace another is an art. Letting go of your intellectual side and embracing the attitude of innocent faith is not difficult, as long as you really desire it.

"Sri Shankara[7] was a Self-realized master. He was also a great scholar with a superb intellect. Through his knowledge and reasoning, he removed many misconceptions about spirituality, and brought to light the right interpretations of the scriptures. At the same time, he had immense faith in what he taught. It was not just because of his intellectual ability to penetrate into the meaning of the scriptures that Shankara was so widely admired and respected, but because he himself was an embodiment of everything he preached. The realization, 'I am That,' is possible only through absolute trust. Without that faith you cannot put the spiritual principles into practice. Intellectual certainty is one aspect of spirituality, while faith is another. Both are important.

---

[7] Sri Shankaracharya, who lived in the 8th century, was a great philosopher and exponent of the Advaita philosophy.

However, the state of Self-realization can be attained through faith alone, whereas intellectual knowledge and reasoning, without faith, cannot take you to the ultimate state."

In a state of rapture

As they were driving, they came to a beautiful, clear blue river beside the road. The river was glistening in the sun, and from the car they could hear the sound of the flowing water. Mother was gazing intently at the river, through the car window. Suddenly She went into a state of rapture shouting, "Hoo… hoo… hoo!" (a sound Mother often produces when in a state of ecstasy). She bounced up and down on the seat like a child, while Her hands formed several *mudras*, one after the other. Seeing Mother's divine, intoxicated mood, the driver slowed down the van. Within a few seconds, Mother went into a deep state of samadhi. Inspired by Mother's spiritual mood, the brahmacharis sang a song called *Prapancha Mengum*, as the van continued to move slowly along the river.

> *O illusory Appearance*
> *Permeating the entire Universe,*
> *O Radiance, won't You dawn in my mind,*
> *And stay there, shining Your light forever?*
>
> *I will drink in Your love and motherly affection,*
> *And be utterly content;*
> *Coming close to You,*
> *Melting into Your divine light,*
> *All my suffering will vanish.*
>
> *For how many days have I been wandering*
> *In search of You, the Essence of everything?*
> *O my Mother, won't You come to me,*

And grant me the bliss of the Self?
O, won't You come?

When the song came to an end, Mother was again in a state of rapture; and in that state She sang the song, *Radhe Govinda Bhajo*. She was laughing loudly as She sang and Her whole body was moving back and forth, as if dancing in tune with the cosmic rhythm; and as She sang Her hands continued to spontaneously manifest divine mudras. Gradually, Mother returned to ordinary consciousness. For a long time they drove in silence, until Mother again began to speak. She told them a story.

Silence is the answer

"Amma has heard this story somewhere. Once, there lived a great master who was renowned for his wisdom and spiritual attainment. He used to give beautiful, deeply inspiring sermons. The people of a certain village cherished a desire to hear the master speak, and invited him to their village. The master accepted their invitation. When he arrived, there where hundreds of people waiting for him.

"After a grand reception, the master stood on a podium to deliver his speech. The crowd was eagerly waiting for him to speak. He said to them, 'My dear brothers and sisters! I feel happy and privileged to be here with you today. But let me ask you something. Do any of you know the subject I am going to talk about?' As a response to his question, the whole audience shouted, 'Yes, we know!' The master paused, looked out at the crowd, smiled, and said, 'Well, then, if you already know everything about it, there is no need for me to say anything, is there?' Without another word he got down from the podium and left the village.

"The villagers were very disappointed. They decided to invite the master again; and again he agreed to come.

"The day arrived and the master was received in the traditional manner. He was about to deliver his speech, when he asked the audience the same question he had asked the previous time. But this time the villagers were prepared. So when he asked, 'Do any of you know the subject I'm going to talk about today?' all the villagers shouted in unison, 'No, we don't know anything!'

"The master paused, and there was a slightly mischievous smile on his face. He said, 'My dear ones, if you don't know anything at all about the subject, then it would be useless for me to speak, wouldn't it?' Before anyone could protest, the master had left. The audience was stunned. They had been so sure that 'no' was the answer the master expected. You can imagine how disappointed they must have felt. However, they refused to give up. They asked themselves, 'If the answer to the Master's question is neither yes nor no, what, then, could it be?' What were they to say to finally benefit from his wisdom? The villagers had a meeting to discuss the matter, and they decided what they would do next time the master asked them the question. They were certain that this time it would work. Once again they invited the master. He arrived on the appointed day. The villagers were both nervous and exited. The master stood up before them, and as usual he asked the same question: 'Brothers and sisters, do you know anything about the subject I wish to talk about?' Without a moment's hesitation, half the crowd shouted, 'Yes!' and the other half shouted, 'No!'

"The villagers then waited expectantly for the master's response. But the master said, 'Well, then, let those of you who know teach those who do not know!'

"This was an unexpected blow to everyone. Before they had time to recover from the shock, the master quietly left the place.

"What were they to do now? The villagers were determined to hear him speak. They decided to give it one more try. They had another meeting. People suggested all sorts of things, but nothing seemed to be the answer. Finally, an old man stood up and said, 'Whatever we answer seems to be wrong, so the next time the Master asks that question, wouldn't it be best if we were absolutely quiet and said nothing?' The villagers agreed.

"The next time the master arrived, he asked the same question as usual. But this time no one spoke. It was so quiet you could hear a pin drop. In the depth of that silence, the master finally began to speak, and the words of his wisdom flowed out towards the villagers."

When Mother had finished the story, Br. Amritatma thought, "The story is beautiful, but what does it mean? It must have a deeper meaning. If Mother would only explain…." Before he had finished formulating the question in his mind, Mother turned to him and said, "The meaning of the story is that only in the depth of pure silence can we hear God's voice. During his first visit, when the master asked if they knew what he was going to speak about, the villagers said, 'Yes, we know.' That is the ego. The thought, 'I know', is the ego speaking. When the intellect (the seat of the ego) is full of information, nothing else can enter into it. The mind that is brimful with intellectual knowledge cannot receive even a drop of true spiritual knowledge. This is the reason why the master did not speak during his first visit.

"During his second visit, the villagers replied to the same question saying, 'No, we don't know anything!' That is a negative statement. A closed, negative mind cannot receive the highest wisdom either. To receive pure knowledge, one has to be wide-open and receptive like an innocent child.

"The third time, they said both yes and no. This exemplifies the doubtful, vacillating nature of the mind. An unsteady, doubting mind is incapable of being open to any real knowledge.

"Finally, when the people kept quiet, the master spoke. Only when the mind stops all its interpretations can we hear the inner voice of God.

"These four responses can be compared to a tumbler that we want to fill with water. The first answer, 'Yes, we know,' is like a tumbler that is already filled to overflowing. There isn't room for another drop. The second response, 'No, we don't know anything,' is like a tumbler turned upside-down. It would be useless trying to pour anything into it. The third response, when the two opposite answers, 'yes' and 'no,' were given, can be compared to a water-filled tumbler mixed with dirt. The water has been contaminated and has lost its purity. Any additional water poured into it would also be spoiled. Only the fourth answer, silence, is like an upright, empty tumbler that is capable of being filled with, and retaining, the water of knowledge.

"To be able to listen to, assimilate, and digest the words of a true master, we need to develop our inner ear. The physical ears are not capable of listening to God. They usually work like two ventilators: the sound comes in through one ear and goes out through the other. We need to have a special 'inner' ear.

"To be able to imbibe the teachings of the master, we have to be open within. We need to develop a special 'womb' to contain the master's teachings. A noisy mind that is full of words should be taught to be silent and to listen intently. Not just a part of you should listen, not just your mind and ears—you should listen with your whole being.

The way to surrender

"Only when Arjuna stopped speaking on the battlefield, did Krishna begin to speak to him. In the beginning Arjuna had countless misconceived ideas. He talked and philosophized endlessly. Finally, he was exhausted and felt utterly helpless. He dropped his weapons to the ground and stood quietly next to Krishna. His bow and arrows symbolize his ego—the intellect, the feeling of 'I' and 'mine', the attitude that 'I' can fight and win. He dropped the ego and stood quietly in a state of utter despair. His worldly knowledge, his royalty, his strength and skills as a great warrior couldn't help him now. He had no choice but to accept his total failure; and, having done so, he exposed his sense of helplessness to Krishna. Only then did the Lord speak, because now Arjuna was open enough to listen. That silent stillness is the state of surrender. Only in the silence of surrender can you truly listen. In that inward silence, when your whole being is still and quiet, surrender takes place. That is why it is impossible to teach anyone how to surrender. It is something that simply happens in the presence of a satguru. The master slowly leads the disciple to this state, by creating the necessary conditions for it to happen.

"When Arjuna demanded to take a look at his enemies, who were eagerly waiting to fight with Krishna and the Pandavas[8]—Krishna, the Universal Being, deliberately placed the chariot in such a way that Arjuna could see Bhisma, Drona, and the other warriors whom he deeply loved and respected. The Lord had slowly created different situations leading up to this finale: Arjuna's self-surrender. This was only one among a chain of circumstances which had been created for this purpose. Krishna knew that what was happening now would bring the whole process to a climax; and this is precisely what happened. Seeing

---

[8] Arjuna and his brothers

there before him on the battlefield the people with whom he was about to fight: his beloved kith and kin and his teachers whom he worshipped, Arjuna was overcome with attachment and fear. He began to speak like someone deeply disturbed, emptying out all that was in his mind, all the knowledge and values he had gathered from the outer world. The Lord allowed him to let it all out, and Arjuna was soon exhausted. He became aware of the state of delusion he was in. He realized that he couldn't find a solution to the extraordinary situation he now had to face. In his state of utter hopelessness and helplessness, he finally surrendered to the Lord. However, it happened only after all his talking had come to an end. From the world of words he slipped into a new world of inner silence, and he was able to listen to Krishna's words of wisdom with his whole being.

"Everyone hopes to succeed in life. A successful person hopes to continue doing well, or even better; there are people who have not yet made it to the top, but they are trying; and there are those who have failed, and yet they continue to hope they will succeed. But all those people are very tense. They experience a great deal of stress and strain. Whether they have failed or succeeded in the past, they have a lot of hopes about the future, and they're always dreaming about it. In the case of such people, surrender will not come easily, for they will be strongly inclined to continue their struggle. On the other hand, a person who finds himself in the same mental state as Arjuna has no choice but to surrender. Such a person feels utterly defeated. In that state there is no longer any question of hope or hopelessness, past and future. You just surrender.

"Only a satguru can lead you to this state. Only in his presence can this happen. Put aside all your logic, interpretations, and explanations, as Arjuna did, because it won't help you in the critical stage when you realize you have failed. That failure is the failure of the ego, the failure of your intellect. Accept your failure and allow yourself to move into a state of inner silence. Then, in that silence you can easily surrender.

"It is when you have tried and failed that you are truly able to surrender. Though you fail time and again, you continue to try until, finally, there comes a point when you accept your failure; you fully experience and understand your incapacity to move forward. It is at that point that you surrender. So keep trying. That ultimate sense of failure must come to everyone, either today or tomorrow.

"All effort comes from the ego. Because the ego is limited, it's capacity is also limited. Utter defeat and failure is therefore bound to happen, sooner or later. When that happens, your mind becomes silent and you surrender. Your whole being turns towards God. It is your efforts that lead you to the state of utter failure, which in turn helps you to surrender.

"Unfortunately, we have a strong tendency to find an explanation for everything. Never accepting our failures, we find some reason or other to justify everything we do. Amma has heard a story.

"A man went into a restaurant and ordered a meal. He was so hungry that as soon as the food was placed on the table before him, he began to eat ravenously, using both his hands. The waiter was puzzled by his strange behavior and asked, 'What are you doing? Why are you eating like that with both hands?' The man replied, 'Because I don't have three hands!'"

Mother continued, "Most people are like that. They are not honest enough to tell the truth or to admit their failures. No matter what happens, they always try to justify their actions."

Mother stopped talking and sat looking out through the car window. It had been a long drive. They had left Garberville at ten in the morning and it was now five o'clock. They were nearing

Mount Shasta. For some time, Mother sat gazing up at the sky. Then the mountain came into view. Mother kept looking intently at some fixed point, either in the sky or on the mountain—no one could tell.

Mount Shasta

When they finally arrived at six o'clock, Mother received a warm welcome by a group of local devotees. Two hours later She was driven to the town where She was to give an evening program of bhajans and darshan. Many people had traveled up from San Francisco to be with Mother. There was a big crowd waiting for Her at the hall. It was located near the source of the huge Sacramento river, which is just a spring of crystal-clear, ice-cold water that pops out of the ground, carrying down the melted snow from the mountains.

After the bhajans, Mother gave darshan to Her children. By the time everyone had gone up to Mother, it was 3 a.m. Despite Her long journey and so many hours of giving darshan, Mother still looked as fresh as a newly blossomed flower.

The lifestyle at Mount Shasta was simple. There were only small, rustic houses with no electricity. But it was quiet and peaceful. People in this area liked to be away from all the noise and bustle of city life. They preferred to be with nature, even though they had relatively few material comforts.

The morning darshan was held on a hill out in the open, against the backdrop of the sacred mountain, which loomed majestically above the scene, silently witnessing the beauty and grace of the Universal Mother blessing its foothills with Her presence. People were sitting around Mother in the chilly morning air, which was permeated with the power of Mother's presence. The day began with meditation, and then Mother gave darshan. Spending the day with Mother in this beautiful landscape was an unforgettable experience for everyone.

A few months earlier, the local devotees had built a small temple for Mother. They now expressed a wish that Mother would hold the next day's darshan inside the temple. When Mother agreed, the excited devotees spent the whole afternoon cleaning and widening the area in front of the little building to enable more people to sit inside.

As Mother walked into the temple the next morning, people were clapping their hands and singing, *Amma Amma Taye*. The joy they felt could clearly be seen on their faces.

O Mother,
Dearest Divine Mother,
Goddess of the Universe,
Who nourishes all creatures,
You are the Primal Supreme Power.

Everything in this world takes place
Because of Your divine play;
Protect me, O Mother.
Without conceiving in the womb,
You have given birth of millions upon millions of beings.

O Sister of Lord Vishnu who rides the bird Garuda,
O Beautiful One,
From the moment of my birth
I have sung Your praises.
You are the Perfect One,
The Primordial Cause,
The Destroyer.

O Mother, You are the goal of my life
O Goddess of the world, don't ignore me!
You are the Goddess Lalita, the Ruler of the world
O Mother, if you cast me into trouble again and again,
Who else will be there to protect me?
O Mother with the enchanting eye,
You are the omnipresent Witness of everything.

Oh Mother,
Dearest Divine Mother…

After the usual ceremonial washing of Mother's holy feet, followed by arati and meditation, Mother began calling people to come for darshan. A little girl pushed her way through the crowd and came up to Mother. She handed Mother a drawing. It was an attempted portrait of Mother. Just below the drawing she had written in a big childish scrawl, "I love you, Amma." Mother looked very moved. She took the picture and brought it up to Her face, touching it to Her forehead as a sign of love and reverence. Mother hugged the little girl and lifted her into Her arms. Holding her close, Mother rocked her back and forth with great affection.

Finally, when Mother wanted to put her down, the little girl refused to let go. Clasping her arms around Mother's waist she said loudly, "No! I want to stay in Amma's lap!" This innocent statement evoked much laughter. Someone shouted, "Yes, that's what all of us would like to do!" Again everyone laughed. Mother also burst out laughing, while the little girl snuggled in Mother's lap with her eyes closed. Eventually, her mother came and managed to coax her away..

The Atman alone is

A devotee asked Mother: "Amma, I have seen you touching your forehead when you receive an offering or a letter from your devotees, as if you were bowing down to it. You did this just now when that little girl gave you her drawing. What is the significance of this?"

Mother: "Children, Amma beholds God in everything. To Amma, there is nothing but God, the Paramatman. The Atman alone is. Amma sees everything as part of the whole, as an extension of Her own Self. Once we experience everything as part of ourselves, how is it possible to ignore anything? How can we consider any living being, or even a non-living object, to be insignificant? In that state there is no sense of otherness: everything is permeated with consciousness.

"Only if we perceive ourselves as separate entities can we ignore others or think of them as insignificant, because then we are identified with the ego—with our anger, hatred, jealousy, judgment, and all the other negative qualities. But when we are one with the Self, we do not place any importance on petty feelings. The ego is not given any importance. We constantly remain within the Self, the very center of existence. It is because we have forgotten our true Self, and because the ego interferes, that a sense of otherness is experienced. At present we are only aware of our small self—we are self-centered. We have to grow out of our self-centeredness and become centered in our true Self, in Brahman, the Absolute Consciousness.

"A person who is poor will strive to get rich; an obese person will try to lose weight; and a person who is sick will do everything he can to find a cure. So there is no question of people not being aware of their limited selves. People are very conscious of their bodies and their physical existence. That is not the problem. The problem is that, at the same time, they don't know anything about the divine inner Self. Once you become aware of the boundless Self, you stop identifying with the small, limited self.

"People have forgotten who they are; that they are the very center of everything, the center of the entire creation. Instead, they identify with something that they are not.

You are the center of the whole show

"Amma will tell you a story. A great party was in progress. It was a wonderful party; everything was perfect, and all the guests were happily enjoying themselves. Around midnight a crazy gatecrasher sneaked into the house and joined the celebration. He approached the host and said, 'What a boring party! What a suffocating atmosphere!' He went on and on about what a terrible party it was in such a convincing way that, finally, the host began to be persuaded. He forgot how much he had been enjoying himself until now and became convinced that it really was a terrible party. He even forgot that he himself was the host! So he said to the gatecrasher, 'You're absolutely right. It's awful! Let's go somewhere else.' 'Yes,' said the gatecrasher. '*I* will organize a fantastic party—it will be my party, and you will be my guest.' The gatecrasher began to promise him all sorts of wonderful, enticing things. They left the party together and went to the gatecrasher's house. It was a dreary place—ugly, dirty, and lifeless, and no one else was there. But the crazy gatecrasher, believing his own illusions of grandeur, kept trying to persuade his guest that the gloomy house was a beautiful mansion and that they were about to enjoy themselves at any moment. 'The fun will soon begin,' he kept saying. But nothing happened.

"In the beginning the man believed him, but then he suddenly returned to his senses. 'Wait a moment!' he exclaimed. 'What is it?' said the gatecrasher, looking worried. 'Oh no!' exclaimed the man. 'What am I doing here in this horrible place? I have forgotten that I am the host of that other wonderful party—that is my home! I have forgotten how much I was enjoying myself there.' Ignoring the gatecrasher's protests, the man walked out through the door and hurried back to his own house. All his friends were still there having a great time; they hadn't even noticed he was gone. He smiled at them and happily rejoined the celebration.

"The entire human race is in a similar position. People have forgotten who they are. We are supposed to be living in our own wonderful home, where we belong, enjoying the splendid celebration of life and creation. Like the host in the story, we are, in fact, the center of it all, but we do not know it. Something has gone terribly wrong. The ego has sneaked in and has lured us into a state of utter forgetfulness, a state of unconsciousness. We have forgotten that we are the host of a glorious celebration. Instead, as if sleepwalking, we have left to join the ego, the 'crazy gatecrasher', at his non-existing party.

"The ego is an outsider. But we, the host, the real center of the wonderful 'party', around whom the whole play of creation is taking place, have forgotten the truth about our real Self. We have mistakenly attached ourselves to the ego, the impostor, identifying with the ego and its distorted views.

"We need to wake up from our stupor and remember that we are the 'host', the very center of creation. Then, we, too, will exclaim, 'Oh no, what am I doing here? I have forgotten that I am the host of that party! That is my home! I have completely forgotten how much I was enjoying myself over there!' Then you will not waste another moment. You will rush back to your real home, and remain within your blissful, joyful Self.

"From your real dwelling place within the Self, you witness everything. Everything revolves around the Self. Everything is great fun. While remaining forever within the Self, you enjoy the whole play.

"Others are also part of the game, but for them it's a play of the ego. Being ignorant, they play the game from within the tight clasp of their egos. Instead of simply witnessing the play, they become entangled in it, identifying with it. The awakened soul, on the other hand, never identifies with the play, though he enjoys taking part in it. For him it is a play of infinite Consciousness. While all the others are playing the game in a state of forgetfulness, as if they were sleepwalking, the one who is centered in the Atman is always fully awake and aware.

"In that infinite play of consciousness, where God is the very center, nothing is insignificant. Everything is permeated with Divinity. Every blade of grass and every sand particle is filled with divine energy. The awakened one thus has an attitude of deep reverence and humility towards all of creation; because once you go beyond the ego, you are nothing—you are infinite nothingness filled with Divine Consciousness. When you have the attitude of constantly bowing down with a feeling of humility towards all existence, that existence flows into you. You experience that everything is part of you, nothing is separate.

"Think of how much you care about yourself. You want to eat good food, live in a wonderful home, sleep in a comfortable bed, travel in a beautiful car, and you don't want anyone to hurt or insult you in any way. You always want to be happy. This is because you love and care about yourself more than anything. Now imagine what will happen when you become one with everything and everyone. You will love, honor, and care about everyone and everything equally, but with infinitely greater depth and power than you have ever loved yourself."

Mother began singing a song called *Devi Jaganmata.*

Hail to the Goddess, the Mother of the world,
The Goddess of Supreme Energy!

O Eternal Virgin,
Doing penance on the shores
Of the blue sea at Kanyakumari,
Come and give me a boon!

O Mother, whose true nature is Light,
And whose exquisite form
Is made of wisdom, truth, energy and bliss!
Aum
Hail to the Mother of the Universe!

A bonus darshan at Mount Shasta

There was no darshan scheduled for the next day. In the morning, Mother was supposed to leave for San Francisco, from where She was to fly to New Mexico the following morning. But Mother decided not to waste the day, and announced that She would be giving darshan one more time at Mount Shasta. Everyone was overjoyed. They had been feeling sad because Mother was leaving.

Once again the devotees prepared the small temple for Mother's darshan.

Mother came at 10 a.m. It was a rainy day, so everyone squeezed into the temple. Before long the little building was completely full.

Even though the Devi Bhava the night before had been very long, Mother looked fresh and radiant as usual. She spent the whole day with the people. Amritatma, who was sitting next to Her, was amazed to see how much Mother gave of Herself, lavishing Her love on each person. Her whole being was present in what She was doing. Through Her every word, look, touch, and smile, Mother poured Herself into the people. Nothing was done in a partial way. Whatever She did at each moment was complete and perfect.

People were glued to Mother's every movement, word, and glance, and to every smile on Her face. No one could bring themselves to leave.

Throughout the day, parents also brought their children up to Mother. The children clearly adored Mother, their faces shining with joy as She loved them, played with them, and joked with them.

To each person who came up to Her, Mother gave a great deal of time and attention. Some people asked questions to clear their spiritual doubts, others asked Her to bless their families or to help them in their careers, while others hoped that Mother could cure their diseases. Many people burst into tears in Mother's lap.

As usual, bhajans were being sung throughout the darshan. Sometimes Mother sang a whole song while a devotee rested in Her lap. Now and then, She went into a deep state of rapture. The temple was filled with an extraordinary feeling of joy and peacefulness. At one point, Mother sang *Mano Buddhya*.

> *I am not the mind, intellect, ego, or memory*
> *I am not the taste of the tongue*
> *Or the senses of hearing, smell, and sight*
> *I am not earth, fire, water, air, or ether*
> *I am Pure Bliss Consciousness*
> *I am Shiva, I am Shiva*
>
> *I am not right or wrong actions*
> *Nor am I pleasure or pain*
> *I am not the mantra or any sacred places*
> *The Vedas, or the sacrifice*
> *I am not the act of eating, the eater, or the food*

I am Pure Bliss Consciousness
I am Shiva, I am Shiva

I have no birth or death
Nor have I any fear
I don't hold any caste distinction
I have no father or mother
Friends or companions
I have no Guru
I have no disciple
I am Pure Bliss Consciousness
I am Shiva, I am Shiva

I have no form
Or movements of the mind
I am the all-pervasive
I exist everywhere
Yet I am beyond the senses
I am not salvation
Or anything that may be known
I am Pure Bliss Consciousness
I am Shiva, I am Shiva

A devotee came up to Mother and asked for a mantra. Mother gave him a mantra, and then, at his request, She spoke about mantras.

The mantra

Mother: "Children, when Amma gives you a mantra, She sows a seed of spirituality within you. She transmits a part of Herself into your heart. But you have to work on it. You have to nurture that seed by meditating, praying, and chanting your mantra regularly, without fail. You have to be totally committed.

"The natural way to get yogurt is by adding a spoonful of yogurt to warm milk. Having added the culture, you let it stand for some time, and thus, all the milk is transformed into yogurt. In the same way, Amma has transmitted part of Herself into you. Now you have to 'let the milk stand'—you have to attain a state of inward stillness by constantly repeating your mantra and doing other spiritual practices. Your entire being will thus be transformed and you will then realize your divine nature."

A young man interrupted:

"Amma, long ago, a spiritual master would put a potential disciple through rigorous tests before he gave him a mantra. Amma, you don't do that. Why do you give us mantras without first testing our competency?"

Mother smiled and replied: "Simply because Amma loves you! How can a mother not want to help her children! However incompetent her children may be, a mother can only be compassionate towards them. Children, you are Amma's own, and Amma wants all Her children to reach the ultimate goal. This is why She gives you a mantra. You don't need to analyze the reason; just make use of the mantra by constantly chanting it, and it will take you to the state of realization.

"The vital force of a perfect master has been sublimated and is completely pure. There is no lust in such a being. He or she is like a vast transformer which can transmit an unlimited amount of power to others. By receiving mantra initiation, you imbibe some of the master's spiritual power. By doing sadhana you can become that pure 'Essence' itself. In other words, you become like the master, or you become one with the master.

"The mantra given by a satguru will take you to the state of the supreme swan, the *Paramahansa*."[9]

---

[9] The ultimate state is symbolically represented by a swan. It is said that the swan can extract milk from a mixture of milk and water. This represents the supreme

As Amritatma was translating, he mispronounced the word "swan", and it sounded as if he was saying "swine." Everyone was wondering what Mother could possibly mean by this. When Amritatma saw the confusion on their faces, he repeated the word several times. The people said, "Swine? What do you mean by swine?" Someone said, "You don't mean a pig, do you?" Amritatma said, "No! No!" Finally, someone figured it out and said, "Oh, you mean swan!" When the misunderstanding was translated to Mother, She laughed so much, Her whole body was shaking.

By this time, almost everyone in the tent knew they wanted a mantra, and Mother was ready to fulfill their wish. When each person had gone up to Her and had received a mantra, Mother continued to speak on the subject.

"To begin with, chant the mantra quietly, while moving your lips. Then chant it mentally. Then with each inhalation and exhalation, chant the mantra until it becomes spontaneous and continuous. You will eventually reach a state of meditation in which the mind becomes still, and the *japa* (repetition of the mantra) will stop of its own accord."

Question: "But Amma, where can we find sufficient time to chant the mantra in the midst of our busy lives?"

Mother: "Children, if you have the determination and sincerely long for it, you will somehow find more than enough time. Just be patient. Amma will tell you a story.

"There was once a very busy businessman who was experiencing a lot of tension and worries in his life. None of the methods he used to try to calm his mind seemed to work. One day he saw a holy man sitting under a tree and decided to approach him for advice.

---

state of being able to discriminate between the Atman and anatman, the eternal Self and the ever-changing body and outer world.

"Bowing down humbly before the master he said: 'Oh Revered One, my mind is filled with tension. I have no peace of mind. Please tell me what I can do to find happiness.'

"The sage replied, 'Try to do some spiritual practices every morning and evening.'

"'But where would I find the time for such things?' exclaimed the businessman. Saying thus, he brought out a bundle of keys from his pocket and dangled them in front of the master. 'Just look at how many keys I have!' he said. 'Each key represents a multitude of responsibilities I have to attend to! So please suggest a much easier path.'

"The master replied, 'All right then, I will initiate you into a mantra. Try to repeat it a few times each day, that's all.'

"'But I don't have enough free time to do even that! Isn't there an easier method?'

"'How far is it from your bed to your bathroom?' asked the mahatma.

"Puzzled by the strange question, the businessman replied, 'About fifteen yards.'

"'In that case, I'm sure you don't have any other work to do when you are walking the short distance to your bathroom. So try to repeat the mantra at least during those few seconds every morning.' And having said this, the mahatma gave the man a mantra.

"The next morning when the man woke up, he remembered to chant his mantra on his way to the bathroom. Then, as he was brushing his teeth, he thought, 'I can chant the mantra a few times now as well.' The same thing happened while he was taking a bath, when he was putting on his clothes, and while driving to work. In fact, many times during the day, he realized that he was free to chant his mantra at least a few times. And as the days went by, he managed to find more and more time to chant his mantra, until it became his habit to repeat it wherever he was, no matter what he was doing. This had a great effect on him. By chanting his mantra he became a changed man. He found the inner peace he needed, and his business also greatly improved.

"Some people want to know the meaning of the mantras. But when you are traveling in an airplane it isn't necessary to know what type of metal the plane is made of, how the instruments work, or who the pilot is. You don't have to know those details. The only important thing is that you reach your destination. By simply repeating the mantra, you will reach the goal.

"The ultimate goal of life is Self-realization. Knowing this, we should try to understand the transitory nature of the world. Then, with strong faith, determination, and full concentration, we should chant our mantra during every possible moment.

"You are trying to cross the ocean of transmigration, the cycle of birth and death. The mantra is the oar of the boat; it is the instrument you use to cross the *samsara* of your restless mind, with its unending thought waves.

"The mantra can also be compared to a ladder that you climb to reach the heights of God-realization.

"The mantra can be chanted anywhere and at any time. You should chant it always—even when you're in the bathroom. If you constantly repeat the mantra, while visualizing the deity that the mantra represents, you yourselves will gradually take on the characteristics of that deity."

Question: "Amma, is it all right to visualize your form?"

Mother: "You can do so if you wish. Amma would be happy if hundreds of people became like Her, because then Amma could serve many more people in the world."

"All your thoughts pass through me"

It was now late in the afternoon. Br. Amritatma was exhausted and was beginning to feel restless. He had been busy the whole day, without a moment's break, translating Mother's answers to all the questions She was asked, and he was also busy giving instructions to those who had received a mantra. But Mother showed no sign of fatigue. She was smiling happily, glowing with Her inexhaustible love and energy. Amritatma wanted to say to Her, "Amma, it's enough! It's 4 o'clock. Why can't you stop?" As he was thinking this, Mother turned to him and said, "How can Amma stop when Her children are crying for help? Son, you should surrender and accept, because that's how real joy is found."

Mother gazed at Amritatma for a moment and said, "Son, every thought of my children passes through me."

At five in the afternoon, Mother finally finished giving darshan and got up. But, before She left, She stayed in the temple a few more minutes and chatted with everyone. They were overwhelmed with gratitude towards Mother for Her compassion.

Finally, at a quarter past five, Mother left. As She walked towards the van, She sang, *Shiva, Shiva, Hara, Hara.*

> *O Auspicious One*
> *Destroyer of the unreal*
> *Who is clothed in the clouds*
> *O Beautiful One*
> *Who is playing the damaru drum*
>
> *Who holds the trident in His hand*
> *Bestowing fearlessness and boons*
> *Who has matted hair locks*
> *And limbs covered with ashes*

Who is adorned with a garland of cobras
And a necklace of human skulls
Who supports the crescent moon on His forehead
And whose eyes are filled with compassion

O Auspicious One
O Destroyer
Great God

When Mother stepped into the van, everyone crowded around it, wanting to catch a last glimpse of Mother before She left. When the van sped away it was still raining, as it had done all day—not a gray, dreary rain, but a cheerful shower dancing on the ground. It was as if nature was reflecting the atmosphere of joy and celebration around Mother, playfully mimicking the outpouring of Her grace with a continuous shower of shining raindrops.

❦❦

Santa Fe

On June 4 Mother arrived in New Mexico, where She was going to spend almost two weeks giving darshan in Santa Fe and nearby Taos. In Santa Fe Mother stayed with Steve and Kathy Schmidt who lived in the countryside just outside the town.

Mother received people in the Schmidt's living room. Though the crowd was small, Mother spent many hours giving darshan.

How to heal the wounds caused by the past

A young man came up to Mother and asked a question: "Amma, many Westerners have been hurt and disillusioned by some of the gurus that have come to the West. In the name of spirituality and the importance of self-surrender, they have exploited the men and women who have sincerely approached them for guidance. They have exploited them financially, sexually, and emotionally. Many have lost their faith in gurus and spirituality because of these incidents. Amma, how can these people overcome their loss of faith, and their fear and suspicion? How can their faith in a guru ever be rekindled?"

Mother: "Only in a *satguru's* (Self-realized master's) presence can the deep wounds of the heart, which have been caused by a false guru, be healed. You may have been with a so-called guru who has hurt you in many ways, but don't ever lose your faith or give up hope. Amma can assure you that the time and energy you have dedicated to your sadhana have not been wasted. The power you have acquired through your spiritual practices is still there, because, unlike material gain, what you have gained through your sadhana cannot be lost.

"When the hurt feelings you harbor deep within are manifested outwardly, they are expressed as anger, hatred, anxiety, and guilt. If your inner wounds are not healed, those negative tendencies will accumulate and grow worse.

"Unfortunately, there are many sincere aspirants who have been deeply hurt by so-called gurus. Amma understands how difficult it must be for a seeker who has been hurt and misled to trust anyone. But complete distrust is not a solution; it will only make you far too negative, which will be the cause of further fear and anxiety. If the wounded seeker should happen to come across a satguru, a truly realized being, the satguru's mere presence, touch, look, and words can heal the inner wounds, no matter how deep they are.

"Children, many of you have deep inner wounds. There is so much pain. Those wounds and that pain give others the power to hurt you, again and again. Words cannot heal you, nor can intellectual knowledge; but the unconditional love and compassion you experience in the presence of a perfect master can heal your wounds, and you will receive the necessary strength to prevent you from being hurt again by anyone. You will no longer be vulnerable because of any psychological wounds, and therefore, no person or situation will have the power to harm you.

"However, before you can remain unaffected by situations, you have to work on removing the existing pain and hurt feelings. But you cannot do it alone. You are a sick patient, so to speak, and you do not know enough about your disease or its treatment. You need a competent healer who is able to penetrate deep within your mind, who can clearly see your problems and remove them. A person with only ordinary eyes cannot help you. Only someone whose inner eye is opened can heal you, and that person is the satguru.

"If you feel you can no longer trust anyone because of your past experiences with a false guru, who will lose by this? Not the true master who is willing to help you. It makes no difference to him whether you surrender to him or not. Being perfectly complete as he is, the satguru has nothing to gain or lose by anything. He doesn't need anyone's praise or adoration. He has no desire for fame, nor does he need any disciples. The master is the wealthiest of all beings, the entire universe is contained within him. He is the master of the universe. His very presence creates a constant wave of circumstances in the disciple's life, which leads to the disciple's transformation. There is no force involved, nor does the master make any claims. If you trust him, you will be greatly benefited; if you don't trust him, you will simply remain as you are.

"Suppose you happen to walk past a garden full of exquisitely beautiful flowers. As you glance at them, a hint of their beauty and scent reaches you. But instead of pausing to enjoy the garden, you ignore it and walk on. Who loses by this? The flowers have nothing to gain or lose. It is you who lose what could have been a precious experience. Whether you care to enjoy them or not, the flowers will continue to manifest their beauty. They are simply offering themselves to the world, without the slightest wish to be praised or adored.

Faith as a whole cannot be lost

"You are asking how to rekindle the faith of those who have lost their faith due to the bitter experiences they have had with other gurus. Children, your faith cannot be totally lost. Faith in someone or something can be lost, but your faith as a *whole* cannot be lost.

"Most people, even after such bitter experiences, decide to get on with their lives. They may have lost faith in spirituality and all spiritual masters, but they haven't lost faith in life itself. After all, one can observe that they are living normal lives; they are working, and many of them are raising families. So, they still believe in many things.

"Very few people believe that spirituality is an important part of life. Even fewer consider it a way of life, the very essence of life itself. The traumatic experiences mentioned in your question would be a terrible blow to anyone. However, there are seekers who have the mental strength, courage, and spiritual understanding to overcome their initial shock and disappointment. They realize that the so-called guru is not a real master, and that they have made an unfortunate mistake in trusting him. After such a deeply distressing experience, the genuine seeker will have the spiritual insight to see what has really happened. He will immediately leave the false guru and search for a perfect master, who can lead him to the goal of God-realization.

"Such a seeker will certainly find a real master, or it would be better to say that the master will find him: the master will appear in his life, without him having to wander about looking for a teacher. This will happen because of the disciple's sincerity and intense longing. It has to happen.

"For the sincere seeker, spirituality is not a minor aspect of life—it is as much a part of him as his own breath. His faith is unshakable. Nothing can destroy his faith in the possibility of experiencing God, or his faith in the great masters who are established in that state.

"Even in the case of people who have been deceived by a false guru and react by turning away from the spiritual path, their faith has not been totally destroyed. Their thirst to know God and to be with a true master still exists deep within them. It may stay hidden for awhile, but it is bound to resurface when the time is ripe. Sometimes this happens when they hear about or see a picture of a great satguru, or if they happen to meet a Self-realized soul. They must have tasted the bliss of God somewhere, either in this or a previous life, and the memory of that experience remains within them, ready to express itself when the proper time comes.

"If you no longer believe in the spiritual masters, it is because you don't believe that spirituality is really necessary, that it's an indispensable part of life. You may think you can live without it—and of course you can to a certain extent—but your life will lack any real charm, richness, joy, or meaning.

"Suppose you were to suffer a great loss in your business. Would you give up hope and stay idle for the rest of your life? No, you'd somehow try to make up for the loss by adopting more effective methods in your business. You may feel disappointed to begin with, but then you'll pick yourself up and start again. You have to, because it's a question of survival, a very real need. So you regain your faith and resume your work. One may ask why people don't have the same attitude towards spirituality and the spiritual masters. If they happen to experience a disappointment on the spiritual path, why don't they feel the urge to continue their pursuit? The answer is that they don't really believe spirituality is an existential problem. The general feeling is that if we lose faith in the spiritual principles, we can live without them, because it won't raise any serious challenge to our lives.

"You may once have believed in spirituality and trusted someone whom you believed to be a real master. Unfortunately, owing to some bad experiences, you lost your faith, and that part of your life was apparently closed forever. But it did not die. A small part of it remains alive. Sooner or later, from that 'green', living area, the shoot of spirituality will again come forth. But only if you meet a satguru can this happen. The satguru will rekindle your faith and heal the wounds and the pain of your past experiences.

"Children, if your faith in God and spirituality was sincere and innocent to begin with, it will eventually return, no matter what you have been through.

"Amma knows many people who have had some bitter experiences with false gurus, which shook them at the very foundation of their faith, and yet they have regained their faith and are again inspired to continue their sadhana. Amma knows that there are many such people present here today. Children, faith in God or in a satguru is the only way to make you truly happy and contented, to make your life a festive celebration.

"If you think about it, it is a form of prejudice to believe that all spiritual masters are false because of the bad experience you may have had with one particular person. Suppose you go to a library. As you enter the place you pick up a book from a shelf, and it happens to be a third-rate novel. You react by walking out of the library saying to yourself, 'Oh no! All the books in this library are worthless!' There may be many good books in there, but your hasty judgment prevents you from discovering and enjoying them.

"Or suppose you enter a shop at the market place. You want to buy some milk, but unfortunately you have mistakenly entered a liquor shop. You immediately get back into your car and drive away saying to yourself, 'How awful! All the shops in this area are liquor shops!' Wouldn't that be foolish? Don't be too quick to judge or to jump to conclusions. Be calm and patient; use your power of discrimination, and be open. Otherwise you are bound to miss many great opportunities in life, many precious experiences."

A satguru is beyond all vasanas

After a short, meditative silence, another question was asked.

"Amma, how can a spiritual master, who is supposed to be beyond all *vasanas* (desires and tendencies), have sexual desires?"

Mother: "A true spiritual master is beyond the mind and the ego. In such a master all sexual energy has been converted into pure *ojas* (vital energy), which he uses for the ultimate good of the world. A satguru is someone who has moved out of the sex center, which is the lowest center of existence, to Sat-Chit-Ananda, which is the highest center of existence.

"All desires exist in the mind. Once the mind is dissolved, there can be no question of having any desires. In that state no trace of desire remains. The so-called gurus who exploit their disciples, sexually or otherwise, or who try to force their ideas on people, are not true masters—far from it. They are still strongly identified with their minds and their desires. A true master will help his disciples to overcome their vasanas. His intention is to make them detached from the grip of the fleeting pleasures and objects of the world. The master teaches the disciple, who until now has been dependent on external objects for his happiness, to become *independent*, finding happiness and contentment in his own Self. However, to be able to lead the disciple from bondage to freedom, the master must himself be completely free from the grip of any vasanas. He must be free from all identification with the mind and its desires. How can he uplift his disciples if he himself is still enslaved by the mind with all its whims and fancies?

"A satguru lives in the world with the selfless intention of leading others out of the dark. Through his words and deeds, he constantly sets an example for his disciples and devotees to follow. He is a living witness to all the sacred scriptures of the world. Such a master is the embodiment of all the divine qualities, such as love, purity, self-sacrifice, patience, and forgiveness. The great masters of the past have given us clear instructions on what a true master is like and what his qualities are. So there is no need to be confused or deluded."

Once acquired, your spiritual power cannot be lost

Question: "Amma, you have mentioned that the spiritual power we gain through spiritual practices cannot be lost, that it will always remain within us. But what about a sadhak who falls from the path? If he, for example, suddenly ceases to be celibate, or if he explodes with anger, doesn't he lose his accumulated energy?"

Mother: "Children, when something like that happens, don't think you will lose all the spiritual power you have gained through hard work. Rather, you are creating another powerful obstacle which will prevent you from progressing spiritually. It will also add to your existing vasanas.

"The purpose of sadhana is to reduce the existing vasanas, and not to add anything to them. When you get angry, it doesn't destroy the power you have accumulated through your sadhana. It does, however, add to your negative tendencies. By creating more negativity, you prolong the journey towards Self-realization, because now additional effort is needed.

"Children, there is no need to lose faith or to feel disappointed. The spiritual energy you have acquired through your sadhana remains within you. Neither your efforts nor the fruit of your actions can be destroyed. If you have done only one second of sadhana, that merit will always be there—and now, you need only do the rest of it. So don't ever give up hope. Don't lose your faith or enthusiasm.

"In worldly life things may go wrong in two ways: There may be complete destruction, or things may turn out the opposite of what you expected. In the first example, suppose you have cultivated a field of rice paddy. You have worked hard and done everything necessary to get a good crop. The plants are growing healthily and you are expecting a rich harvest. But the night before the harvest, there is a terrible storm and the entire crop is destroyed. In this case, you have to start the process of sowing and cultivating all over again.

"In the second example, you have enrolled your son at college. You are expecting him to study hard, to get high marks, and to pass with honors; but all your expectations come to naught when he falls into bad company. He doesn't even bother to appear for his exams and is finally expelled. He ends up ruining his life. So things can turn out very differently from what you expect. However, this is not the case with spirituality. If you have done even one minute's worth of sadhana, the power you have thereby gained will stay within you; it can never be destroyed; that minute will be stored deep within you and can never be lost or dissipated, not even after several lifetimes. Unlike the effort you put forth to accomplish worldly or material goals, spiritual sadhana can never be done in vain. Your actions have to bear fruit.

"If you remember God or if you do your sadhana for just one second, it can never be wasted. The merit you gain will stay within you, and will inevitably come forth, like an ungerminated seed that is still fresh and alive. If you have called God with genuine faith and surrender even for a second, it must be rewarded. Those moments when you remembered God will remain within you and will manifest at the right time.

"Children, stay in the bus until you reach your destination. You may see beautiful, tempting scenes along the way. Enjoy them if you wish, but do so without getting off the bus. Always remember your goal. Once the destination has been reached, you can alight from the bus, because then the means (faith or religion) by which you have traveled is no longer needed—you have gone beyond that. As you dwell in the beyond, you can return if you wish, staying in the world to uplift others. On the other hand, you don't have to come back at all; you can simply dissolve into the infinite."

In Taos Mother stayed with a woman who had a black Labrador and two parrots. Mother enjoyed playing with the dog. Like all creatures, the dog was very drawn to Mother and approached Her as soon as it saw Her. Mother would throw a stick across the garden, and the dog would dash off and retrieve it, wildly wagging its tail as it brought the stick back to Mother, to be rewarded with Mother's delighted laughter and an affectionate pat.

The two parrots lived in a cage outside, at the entrance of the house. Whenever Mother came back from darshan, She would stop at the cage and talk to the birds, while She fed them a handful of nuts. Mother looked at the parrots with great pity and said, "I know how painful it must be for you to be in that cage; how you long to be free and fly through the sky where you belong."

Mother couldn't bear to see birds being kept in cages. Once, when Mother was visiting Her ashram in Reunion, Swami Premananda, a native of Reunion, who was in charge of the ashram, proudly showed Mother a small aviary filled with lovebirds which someone had donated. But instead of being pleased with the gift, Mother was heartbroken when She saw the little creatures trapped in the aviary, flying from one end to the other. She told Swami Premananda that no one in any of Amma's ashrams should ever have birds in cages. She said, "Look, my son, a sannyasi is supposed to feel great empathy towards all creatures. He should feel the pain and the sorrows, not only of human beings, but of animals, birds, plants, and everything throughout creation. These little birds are suffering. They belong to their own world. We have taken away their freedom which is so valuable to them."

Understanding his mistake, Swami Premananda apologized to Mother, and a few days later, he gave the birds away.

❦❦

Boulder

Deal with the present, not with the past

A man came up to Mother and asked a question: "Mother, can you tell me about my past life?"

Mother lovingly patted his back and said, "It is the present that needs to be solved, and not the past. What is happening now is far more important than what has happened before. Only by taking care of the present moment will all your questions and problems come to an end. It is meaningless to look back and try to find out about your previous lives—that is not important. Everything in your present life is the result of the past. Deal with the present; make the very best of each moment, and everything will be all right.

"You are already carrying a heavy burden. You have a tremendous amount to unload. By learning about your previous lives, you will only add more to your existing burden. Amma could tell you who you were, but She will not do so because it would only harm you. It wouldn't serve any purpose. Amma would never do or say anything that could harm Her children. Her purpose is to help you to grow and to open up, not to close down.

"Suppose Amma were to tell you about your past life: who you were, what you were doing, etc. What if you were to discover that some of the people who are with you now, or someone who is very close to you, have harmed you in a previous life? It would cause unnecessary turbulence in your mind.

"A person may discover that their husband or wife has hurt them deeply in the past, or they may have hated someone who they are very fond of now. Why would you want to recall such things? It would only be destructive.

"Even though Amma knows everything about your previous lives, She prefers not to disclose it. You have come to Amma so that the wounds of the past can be healed, and not to create more wounds. The sole aim of a satguru is to pull you out of the quagmire of the past, and not to make you return to it. Your past is the cause of your suffering. The master will see to it that you do not have to suffer again. He wants to take you beyond all suffering.

"Amma knows a woman who was told by a psychic that she had been the cause of her husband's death in a previous life. The psychic told her that she had accidentally given her husband the wrong medicine which had suddenly killed him. Having been told this, she suffered terribly and ended up having a nervous breakdown. So, if this is what the past can do to us, why should we know about it? Of course, there have also been many happy events in the past, but people have a tendency to brood on the painful and depressing incidents, rather than the pleasant ones.

"For a human being to be transformed and to transcend all imperfections and limitations, the past has to die. Everyone has the capacity to do this, provided they have the right determination. Forget who you were or what you may have done in the past. Focus on what you would like to *be*; and then, while you are doing whatever is necessary to attain the goal, let go of the future as well. Who or what you may have been until now is of little importance. The past can be compared to a graveyard; and it wouldn't be wise to live in such a place, would it? Forget your past. Remember it only when you really need to do so, but don't settle down in it.

"The story of Valmiki, the first poet, who wrote the great epic, *Srimad Ramayana*, is a great example of how it is possible to completely die to the past, no matter how negative one's actions may have been.

"Ratnakaran was a robber. He supported his wife and three children by robbing travelers who passed through the forest where he lived. He was a ruthless man, who never thought about God, morality, or ethics.

"One day, the seven *rishis* (great saints) happened to pass through the forest. As usual, Ratnakaran jumped out in front of the travelers, brandishing his knife, and threatened to kill them if they didn't surrender their belongings. The rishis, who had realized the imperishable Atman, and were ever established in the Supreme Truth, were unperturbed by the robber's threats and remained perfectly serene. They said to him, 'We are not afraid of death. We will give you whatever we have; but before we surrender everything, we would like you to answer just one question.' Ratnakaran agreed to their request. The saints asked him to tell them for whom he was doing all those terrible deeds. 'For my wife and children,' he replied. The saints asked him, 'Are your wife and children also willing to take upon themselves a share of your sins?' Ratnakaran was perplexed by this. He wanted to go and ask his wife and children. The rishis gave him their word that they wouldn't move from the spot until he returned. Quickly, the robber ran to his house and asked his wife if she was prepared to share the consequences of the evil actions he was committing to support her. She answered, 'No! You alone will have to suffer the fruits of your actions!' Ratnakaran turned to his children, hoping that at least they would be sympathetic towards him. But they all refused to take upon themselves a share of his sins. Ratnakaran was deeply shocked. He ran back to the rishis, who were patiently waiting for him, and fell at their feet seeking their forgiveness. He completely surrendered to them. With great compassion, they counseled him, initiated him into a mantra, and advised him to do tapas (penance) until he realized God. Ratnakaran sat down right there and then in the forest, and sitting absolutely still, like a rock, he immersed himself in meditation. For years, he stayed there and did severe austerities, until one day, the rishis passed by again; and they remembered their encounter with Ratnakaran. They felt a wonderful serenity in the atmosphere. They found him in deep meditation, completely covered by a termite nest. He had been doing intense tapas and had attained the ultimate state of realization.

"Having aroused him from his state of absorption, the rishis instructed him to go out into the world and sanctify it with his presence, words, and deeds. Because he was sitting in a termite nest, which is known as *valmikam* in Sanskrit, the rishis named him Valmiki.

"This story tells us that it's possible to let go of the past, to leave it behind and move on to an entirely different realm of consciousness. The past is of the mind; it belongs to the world of thoughts and actions. From the mental plane it is possible to ascend to the highest plane, the plane of Truth, provided you have the necessary determination and detachment. From the world of thoughts, you reach a state of no-thought; and from action you move to freedom from action. You transcend to a state of no-mind. Out of compassion, you may then choose to continue to live in the world, blessing and benefiting all beings.

"That one negative response from his wife and children was enough to transform the life of Ratnakaran, the robber. But more than anything, it was the grace and the blessings of the rishis that helped him to realize the error and futility of the life he had been leading, and which raised him to a different level of understanding. It was through their grace that the perfect situation was created which enabled him to surrender.

"Within that short period of time, his whole outlook on life underwent a transformation. He came to see how meaningless human relationships can be, and the shallowness of worldly so-called love. Though it goes without saying that it was unrighteous to live as a robber, he had nevertheless worked hard, day and night, risking his life for his family. When he then heard them so mercilessly reject him, thinking only about themselves, without the slightest sympathy for him, he had a sudden revelation and another world opened up before him. When this happened, he could simply lay aside his great burden of fear, worries, and attachments. Until then, he had believed that his family loved him, that they would support him under all circumstances; and then he suddenly heard them say no, that they would turn their backs on him when the time came. That 'no' was a form of shock treatment that opened a new gate of awareness, through which he suddenly saw life from an entirely different angle. His new understanding helped him to surrender to God, to simply let go of his mind, of his past, and to be at peace. His terrible past disappeared, and a new man was born. The cruel, limited man was dead, and a new, deeply compassionate soul was born.

"Everyone can be transformed like this. The path of spirituality is not just meant for a select few—it is for everyone. However, grace and the willingness to surrender are the most important factors; and when these two factors are combined, a transformation takes place: both the past and the future disappear, and you are fully present in your heart, abiding in the Self."

Mother sang the song, *Krishna, Krishna, Radha, Krishna*.

Krishna Krishna Radha Krishna
Govinda Gopala Venu Krishna
Mohana Krishna Madhusudana Krishna
Mana Mohana Krishna Madhusudana Krishna
Murare Krishna Mukunda Krishna

How to recognize a true master

Mother was giving darshan in the round dome at the Lama Foundation in the mountains above Taos. While holding someone in Her arms, She was blissfully singing, *Hey Giridhara Gopala*. Everyone participated with great feeling, responding to each line as Mother sang:

O Giridhara
Protector of the cowherds
Beloved of Lakshmi
Destroyer of the demon Mura
O Sweet One
Enchanter of the mind

O Son of Nanda
Beautiful form
Who sports in Vrindavan
Who plays the flute
O Protector of the sages

O Giridhara
Who wears the Kaustubha gem

And a pearl necklace
Who plays in Radha's heart
Who uplifts the devotees
O Baby Krishna

O Protector of the cowherd boys
Playmate of the gopis
Who lifts the Govardhana Hill
O Son of Nanda
Butter stealer

Someone began talking to Mother about how deluded people are in the world today. Mother listened to him patiently, and then She said, "Yes, son, you are right. In our modern society people are almost blind. Seeing everything only from an external viewpoint, they have lost their clarity of vision. Their way of seeing and evaluating everything is very superficial. They don't perceive things as they really are. We live in a society that is so unaware, it is half asleep.

"Amma has heard a story. One day a man walked into a gift shop looking for a unique present to buy for someone. As he browsed through the shop he was surprised to see a human skull in a glass case. He was even more surprised to see that the price of the skull was 25,000 dollars. He couldn't believe it when he saw another skull in an adjoining glass case, with a price tag that said 50,000 dollars. With great curiosity, he asked the shopkeeper why the skulls were so expensive. The shopkeeper said, 'Sir, the larger skull is the skull of the first ruler of our country. Being such a unique and precious item, surely you can understand why the price is so high.'

'Yes, I understand,' said the customer. 'But could you please tell me why the smaller one is twice as expensive?' Coolly, the salesman replied, 'Oh, the smaller one! Well, that is also the first ruler's. It was his skull when he was young.'

"The man said, 'O really? How wonderful! I'll take that one!'"

When the laughter had subsided, another question was asked.

"Amma, what is a true spiritual master, and how does one recognize such a master?"

Mother: "A certain intellectual understanding of spirituality is necessary for a seeker to be able to recognize a true master. Of course, one of the criteria is the spontaneous love and attraction one feels towards the master. A satguru is irresistible; people are drawn to him like iron filings to a powerful magnet. The relationship between a real master and disciple is incomparable—there is nothing like it. It has a permanent effect on the disciple. In that relationship the disciple can never come to any harm.

"However, when you feel drawn to someone whom you believe to be a true master, it is very important that you use your power of discrimination. You may feel spontaneously drawn to that person, but as you are not yet established in the state of real wisdom, your feelings are not necessarily to be trusted. You may simply be mesmerized by that person's powers, believing that he can fulfill your needs and desires. As long as your intuition is not a real, integral part of your nature, your feelings are not always to be trusted.

"Think of how many painful psychological blows you have received in your life. Eventually, you become a big walking wound. Why? Because of your wrong judgment. You have failed to use your power of discrimination. An aspect of *karma* is certainly involved here, but remember that however powerful your past may be, how you deal with the present moment is much more important because that is what determines your future.

"If a person boasts of being a guru, without being established in God-consciousness, he will only hurt people through his thoughts and actions. He may talk, walk, and look like a realized master—but see if he loves everything in creation equally and unconditionally and is truly compassionate. If not, be alert, for he is undoubtedly still identified with the ego. Just to catch disciples he may conceal his ego and act innocently. But once he has caught you, he will begin to exploit you and hurt you, creating deep wounds within you.

"Don't get excited if you meet somebody who claims to be a Self-realized master, because people who make such claims can be dangerous. First of all, when one attains the state of supreme realization, one loses oneself in the ocean of Sat-Chit-Ananda. You lose your limited, individual self, and there is no one to claim or declare anything. You simply merge into the infinite ocean of bliss and, instead of speaking about it, you prefer to be silent. However, a realized soul sometimes does speak out of love and compassion for the people. But he would never announce, 'I am Self-realized! I'll take you to God, on the condition that you surrender to me!'

"An authentic master won't do anything in particular to attract anyone's attention, but people will nevertheless be drawn to him. His love, compassion, and serenity spontaneously flow from him, just as rain pours out of a cloud, or water flows forth in a gushing river. Those who are thirsting will be drawn to the water.

"If you are sincere, dedicated, and have enough yearning, you will find the perfect master and he will heal your wounds. Your genuine longing to realize God will lead you to a satguru; or rather, the satguru will appear in your life.

"However, be careful when you enter spiritual life. There are people out there who are good at using flowery, persuasive words, who won't hesitate to make all sorts of claims. Examine such a person and see if he radiates divine love and peace.

"This doesn't mean that you shouldn't listen to any spiritual talks given by scholars. It's all right to do so, but always remember to be cautious and alert. Watch your mind and emotions. Don't allow yourself to be deluded by false claims and promises. That is why Amma says you should have a basic understanding about spirituality, what it really is, and what to look for in a true master.

If you see someone who constantly radiates divine love and compassion, and deep immeasurable peace; someone with an attitude of humility and profound reverence towards every aspect of creation—that is where you need to go. Divine love cannot be imitated. A person who hasn't yet reached the goal may talk like one who is realized, but he cannot possibly love or be as compassionate as a Self-realized being.

"Only a lighted oil-lamp can light another lamp. An unlit lamp cannot light anything. The lighted lamp can continue to light any number of lamps, and yet its flame will remain as full and as bright as ever, without losing the slightest fraction of its power. In the same way, only a jivan mukta, a Self-realized master, can awaken the Divinity within you. He is the blazing lamp that can kindle as many unlit lamps as he wants, and yet he remains ever perfect and complete.[10]

"Once you have attained the state of God-consciousness, peace and compassion will inevitably follow; because peace and compassion are as inseparable from God-consciousness as the light from a lamp, or the fragrance from a flower. Once the lamp is lit, it has to shine; and once the flower opens up, it will inevitably spread its fragrance. Likewise, when your heart blossoms into Divinity, peace and compassion become part of you like a shadow, and you cannot avoid your own shadow. So look

---

[10] "Just as one lamp lights another lamp, the guru imparts the knowledge that everything is Brahman—the Brahman that is imperceptible, eternal, the highest, without form or attributes."—Guru Gita

for a master who constantly radiates divine love, compassion, and peace towards everyone equally—towards all of creation. For that is what a true master is like."

The embodiment of our noblest values

Question: "Amma, some say that a master must abide by certain moral and ethical values in his own life. Others disagree about this. What is your opinion?"

Mother: "A true master will always set an example for his disciples to follow. He is the embodiment of our noblest values. Amma would say that a satguru, even though he is beyond all laws and limitations, must strictly adhere to moral and ethical values. As long as a master remains in his body, serving society, he has to abide by certain fundamental moral and ethical values; for only then can he be an example to others. If the guru says, 'Look, I am beyond everything, and therefore I can do whatever I please! Just obey me and do as I tell you,' it can only harm the disciple. It could even cause the disintegration of society. An authentic master would never make such declarations, because it would be a sign of arrogance. Such a statement in itself implies that the sense of 'I', the ego, is still very much present. A true master is exceptionally humble. He has the attitude of bowing down before everything, allowing pure existence to flow into him and take complete possession of him. The great masters have no sense of ego at all.

"A genuine master is the embodiment of humility. In him you can observe true surrender and acceptance, and thus you are given a real example that you can relate to. Only in the presence of a fully surrendered soul can the disciple spontaneously and effortlessly surrender, without the slightest feeling of there being any force involved.

"To force the disciple in any way would be harmful and would, if anything, impede the disciple's development. Real surrender is something that happens naturally within the disciple. A change takes place inwardly. There is a change in his perception and understanding, and in the attitude behind his actions. The whole focus of his life changes.

"Also, a master wouldn't be setting a good example if he were to proudly declare, 'I am Self-realized,' or, 'I am beyond everything.' If there is any sense of 'I' present, the person is not realized. Self-realization is the total absence of 'I' and 'mine.' It can be compared to being the boundless sky or open space. Does space have any sense of 'I'? No, it just is. It is simply *present*. Does a rain cloud or a flower have any sense of 'I'? No, not at all. Each exists as an offering to the world. Similarly, a true master, who is established in the Self, offers himself to the world. All the great masters of the past, the ancient saints and sages, were perfect living examples of our highest and noblest values.

"There are people who say, 'Why quote or follow the ancients?—after all, they lived eons ago.' They say, 'Spirituality and the spiritual masters have to change and become more flexible, because the world we are living in today is completely different.' Those who say this should understand that there is only one Truth. People may talk about the Truth in different ways, but the experience is one and the same. The Truth has already been explained. There is no new Truth. Asking for a new truth would be childish; it could be compared to a child at school saying to his teacher, 'All the teachers keep telling us that three plus three is six. I'm bored hearing the same old answer again and again. Why can't you give us a new answer, and make three plus three equal something else for a change?'

"No, that isn't possible. Someone may present it in a different way, but you can't invent a new Truth for your convenience.

Even if the guru is beyond the body and devoid of all human weaknesses, the disciples are not. They are still identified with the body and the ego. So they need a living example, an embodiment of all the divine qualities, as a reference to hold on to. The disciples draw their inspiration from the master. A true master, therefore, places great importance on morality and ethics; and he himself strictly adheres to those values, to set an example and to inspire his disciples.

"Of course, the customs, ethics, and morality of different nations may differ. There are, however, certain principles that are universal, that have been shared by people throughout the centuries. For example, the principle of truthfulness has always been applicable to every individual, society, and nation. Truth, peace, love, selflessness, self-sacrifice, and humility are all universally applicable values."

Ambrosial rice water

The first Devi Bhava in Santa Fe was about to take place in Steve and Kathy Schmidt's living room. Gayatri came up to the Schmidts and offered them a cup containing plain *kanji* (rice) water that Mother had drunk from. Both Steve and Kathy took a sip. They immediately felt the effect of the *prasad*. Steve, as he later told Br. Amritatma, was suddenly intoxicated with bliss and felt completely detached from the busy scene around him. Kathy reacted by sitting down in a corner and closing her eyes. She sat like that for several hours, experiencing a profound feeling of peace and joy, while oblivious to the divine play happening around her. For many hours the couple remained in that state. The house was filled with devotees who had come for the Devi Bhava. But as the two hosts were absent from this world due to having tasted the ambrosial kanji water, there was a lot of confusion to begin with, since no one was available to take care of things. This was Steve and Kathy's first experience of Mother's divine power.

⫷⫸

Chicago

The true jnani

Mother was giving darshan at the Hindu temple of greater Chicago. She was singing a song called *Rama Nama Tarakam,* while a devotee rested in Her lap.

The name Rama takes us
Across the Ocean of Transmigration
It gives us both material prosperity and Liberation

That Name was enchanting to Sita
It is the Support of the whole world
And is being worshipped and sung by Shiva and other gods

Rama Hare, Krishna Hare!
I constantly worship Your Name
To cross the ocean of worldly existence
We know no other means than the Names of the Lord

When the song came to an end Mother raised the devotee from Her lap. He lifted his head like someone emerging from another world. There was an expression of deep bliss on his face. As the darshan continued an Indian Brahmin scholar asked Mother a question: "There are certain jnanis (perfect knowers of the Self) who don't perform any actions. They just seem to be blessing people without doing anything. Amma, could you please explain this?"

Mother: "What makes you think *anughraha* (blessing) is so insignificant? The entire universe with all its beauty is a blessing. To be given a human birth is a rare blessing. A jnani blesses people by giving them peace, happiness, and prosperity. Who else could do this but a true jnani? No one in the world, except a person who is one with God, can give such blessings. The grace of a true saint is all-encompassing, it touches the person's life as a whole, making all the different aspects of his life blossom.

"You say that a jnani doesn't do anything. By this, do you mean a well read, scholarly sort of person who calls himself a jnani? Such a one will perhaps do nothing but say, 'I am Brahman'—but a true jnani will always be active in some way, benefiting the world with his presence, words, and actions. Even if the jnani doesn't do any physical work and, from an ordinary person's viewpoint, seems to be doing nothing, he is, in fact, blessing people by his presence. He doesn't have to do any *yagas* or *yagnas* (ritual sacrifices) to bring about a blessing, because his life itself is a sacrifice. Through him flows the grace, glory, and infinite power of God. Indeed, the true jnani is God. That's why people inevitably flock to him, even if he tries to stay away from them. So one cannot judge and say that the jnani isn't doing anything, just because one may see him being physically inactive.

"However, a jnani usually sets an example by being physically active. As for the exceptions to this rule, the jnanis who seem to be doing nothing—an ordinary person cannot even begin to comprehend what such beings are giving to the world.

"Lord Krishna was a perfect knower of the Self. He was exceptionally dynamic, constantly engaged in different actions. He was perfect in every field of action. But although unequaled, Krishna is just one example. There are many great souls who have set a perfect example and have benefited the world immensely by their actions.

"Jivan mukti, liberation from bondage to the cycle of birth and death, is not something to be attained after death, nor is it to be experienced or bestowed upon you in another world. It is a state of perfect awareness and equanimity, which can be experienced here and now in this world, while living in the body. However, the great masters sometimes impart knowledge of the Self to some of their disciples at the time when the disciples leave their body (*videha mukti*). Having come to experience the highest truth of oneness with the Atman, such blessed souls do not have to be born again. They merge with the infinite Consciousness.

"Once jivan mukti is attained, you do not feel as if you are being separated from your body at the time of death, or that you are losing your sense of identity, because, even before the death of the body, your identification with the body has ceased to exist. In other words, you are dead to the body while still living in this world. This supreme state is called moksha, liberation from all attachments to the body.[11] This ultimate goal is to be reached in this life itself.

"The Atman alone is the subject, the One who sees—the Seer. Everything else—that which is seen—is the object. The meaning of *Atma jnana* (knowing the Self) is that the Atman knows the Atman, the Self experiences the Self. The Self cannot be known or experienced by anything other than the Self, dwelling within the Self. If the Atman could be known in any other way, the Atman would only be the object, like any other object. There would then have to be something separate from the Atman with which to perceive the Atman. No, the Atman cannot be seen or known by anything separate from itself; for only the Self is the true 'I', the One who sees everything—the 'Experiencer.' Experiences change, but the Experiencer—the Substratum of all experience—remains one and the same. There is nothing that can know the Atman

---

[11] When Amma refers to the body here, the mind is also implied.

except the Atman itself—the subject knowing the subject. This is what it means to know the Self. So, if someone thinks he has known the Self, understand that he has not known it, because the Self is not an object that can be known; it is the Self knowing or experiencing the Self.

"The ultimate state of knowledge of the Self isn't really an experience; rather, it is a state of *experiencing*—unbroken and everlasting."

⧼⧽

Madison

In Madison, Mother stayed with David and Barbara Lawrence, who were old friends of Nealu's. They were both very devoted to Mother. Their daughter, Rasya, later became deeply attached to Mother and moved to Her San Ramon center.

Shraddha

One evening, when Mother got into the car to go to a program, Gayatri, who was putting Mother's things in a basket to bring to the car, was delayed, so that Mother had to wait for her. When she came running to the car, Mother scolded her for her lack of shraddha.

On the way to the program, Mother said, "Amma doesn't want anyone to serve Her, nor does it matter to Her how you behave; but a spiritual aspirant should be alert and vigilant in all her actions. Shraddha entails both love and faith. When you have love and faith, alertness in all your actions will automatically follow.

"Life brings unexpected experiences. Unless we are alert and vigilant at every moment, we cannot overcome those experiences and face them boldly. An individual's situation in life is like that of a soldier in a battlefield. You can imagine how alert and watchful a soldier has to be in the midst of a battle. An attack could come from any direction. If he isn't extremely alert and constantly on the watch, he could be killed. In the same way, life can bring you any kind of experience at any given time. You need a great deal of shraddha to be able to welcome those experiences and to stay unperturbed in all circumstances. This is what spirituality teaches us. To a spiritual seeker, nothing is more important than shraddha. Don't think that Amma is fussy about small things. Amma is simply trying to help you develop that all-important quality. Even while performing the smallest and seemingly most insignificant action, you need to have shraddha."

Later that night, Mother talked to the brahmacharis about Gayatri. She talked about her with great tenderness. She said, "Amma knows that Gayatri is feeling sad. She may think that Amma is angry with her; it may appear that way, but Amma isn't angry at all. Amma's heart melts when She thinks of Gayatri's self-lessness and sincerity, and how extremely hard she works." There was intense love and compassion in Mother's voice as She spoke.

In Madison Mother visited a home for handicapped children. Mother spent a lot of time with the children, giving each child a great deal of attention, inquiring about their condition, holding them in Her arms, caressing them, joking, and playing with them. The children were enchanted by Mother. Like all children, they immediately took to Her, feeling instinctively that She was their own. As Mother was about to leave, a little girl, who was sitting in a wheelchair, clutched hold of Mother's sari and wouldn't let Her go. Mother held the girl close to Her, stroked her hair, and said, "My child, Amma isn't going anywhere. Amma will always be with you. Amma is with you every single moment." The little girl seemed comforted by this. She grinned happily and let go of Mother's sari.

Peace comes after pain

On the way to a program, Mother asked Br. Rao (Swami Amritatmananda) to get into the car. He had been feeling sad because he wasn't able to spend much time with Mother due to the busy schedule. On the way, Mother spoke to him about pain and joy.

Mother: "Inner peace always follows in the wake of pain. To reach the state of joy, you first have to experience pain. Pain in the beginning and lasting happiness at the end is far superior to happiness in the beginning and long-lasting pain at the end. Pain is an unavoidable part of life. Without having suffered in some way, you cannot experience any lasting peace or happiness.

"This is also applicable to worldly life. Suppose you wish to become a great singer. If this is your goal in life, how can you expect to achieve it without first undergoing the necessary voice training? You should be able to master the most intricate and subtle tones, vibrations, and variations with your voice, traveling smoothly from the lowest to the highest keys. How would this be possible without training the voice properly under the strict guidance of an expert singing teacher? This training is the pain you have to undergo at the beginning before you can become a great maestro. Pain at the beginning is the tapas you have to do, the price you have to pay, for the happiness you enjoy in life. The intensity of the pain varies according to the measure of happiness you seek. Because spiritual bliss is, by far, the greatest joy of all, the intensity of the tapas that is required, or the price you have to pay for that bliss, is also the greatest. You have to dedicate your whole life towards that end.

"In some parts of India, especially in Tamil Nadu, people eat the extremely bitter neem (margosa) flower on New Year's Eve. There is another celebration at the end of the year called Pongal, on the day the sun touches the tropic of Capricorn. On this day, people traditionally chew sugarcane. There is a great deal of symbolism in all the Hindu celebrations. In these two particular examples, chewing the bitter neem flower symbolizes the acceptance of life's bitter experiences from the very first day of life. Life involves many hardships and misfortunes. We should learn to accept and even welcome them wholeheartedly; to be patient, enthusiastic, and optimistic, never allowing ourselves to be mentally weak or disappointed. Only then can we progress towards the real goal of life—the sweet bliss and joy of immortality. This is symbolized by eating sugarcane at the end of the year.

"Some form of pain awaits you in every area of life and in every field of action. Without accepting the pain and going beyond it, you cannot experience the joy and peace that is available as the end result of the pain you go through. By learning to accept the pain of life, you can truly enter into the joy of life.

"Only love can make you open up into God-consciousness. The whole of life is a lesson of acceptance.

"The presence, love, and touch of a divine soul has a great effect on people; it makes them so receptive that they open up.

"There is an incident in the *Ramayana*, which describes how the presence and the mere touch of a great soul can create this receptivity. This incident also explains how inner peace comes after painful experience.

"The date had been set for Sri Rama's coronation. But unfortunately, it didn't take place due to the intervention of Kaikeyi, Rama's stepmother, who at this point demanded the two boons that had once been promised her by her husband, King Dasharatha, who was Rama's father. She demanded that her own son, Bharatha, be crowned as king instead of Rama, and that Rama be sent into exile in the forest for fourteen years. King Dasharatha, who was deeply attached to Rama, was so shocked by his wife's demand that he collapsed. He pleaded with her to change her mind, but the queen was adamant and told him it was his duty as king and the father of Rama, who was the very embodiment of dharma (righteousness), to keep his promise and to implement it immediately. Dasharatha was in a hopeless situation. But Rama, who was the Lord Himself, calmly accepted it. He willingly agreed to leave Ayodhya and go to the forest, allowing his brother Bharatha to accede to the throne. Rama, who was beyond all attachments, showed no sign of anger or disappointment. He was the same calm, balanced Rama as ever.

"But Lakshmana, Rama's brother and faithful servant, who loved the Lord more than anything in the world, became enraged at the news of Rama's impending exile. When Lakshmana found out that Kaikeyi was behind it, his anger knew no bounds. He accused his father of being 'henpecked and unjust.' He wanted Rama's consent to have Kaikeyi and their father imprisoned. He wanted to capture the kingdom for Rama and have Him crowned as the rightful king. Lakshmana was fuming with anger. No one could console him. Rama kept quiet and simply watched as His brother screamed and shouted with rage, challenging their father, until he was finally exhausted. At this point, Rama, who until now hadn't said a word, went up to his brother. He gently touched him and said: 'My child.' That was all that was needed. Those two, simple words and that caress had an immediate effect on Lakshmana. It awakened the child within him. He became absolutely calm and composed, and all his anger vanished. Such is the power of the word and touch of a Self-realized master. It made Lakshmana as peaceful and open as a child before Rama. Rama then began to counsel him, giving him some profound spiritual instructions that went straight to his heart. Before that point, Rama didn't go near Lakshmana or say a word to him. He waited patiently for Lakshmana to go through all that pain and anger, and then He created the perfect opportunity to teach him. Had Rama spoken to his brother before then, when Lakshmana was still raging with anger, his spiritual teachings would have gone straight over Lakshmana's head. So the whole situation, from beginning to end, was created by Lord Rama. If Rama had protested against His father's decision, this opportunity could not have come to pass.

"There are, of course, many reasons on many different levels for everything that happened in the *Ramayana*.

"Rama was the Universal Power in human form. Had he so wished, He could have defeated his opponents in less than a moment and recaptured the kingdom. It was his acceptance of the situation that caused Lakshmana to explode in a fit of rage. But that explosion helped Lakshmana to exhaust all the stagnant negative energy which had been lying dormant within him. Above all, the grace behind Rama's words and divine touch healed Lakshmana and transformed him into a vessel fit enough to receive Rama's spiritual instructions. But before Lakshmana opened up, he had to pass through the painful experience of rage and despair. So, peace and relaxation always follow in the wake of pain and effort. Rama, the perfect master, created the situation by his divine sankalpa for the sake of his beloved brother and disciple.

"It should be mentioned, however, that this situation was specifically suited for Lakshmana in the controlled conditions of his master's presence; otherwise you may think there is no need to control your anger or to be aware of its largely negative aspect. To just explode in a fit of rage whenever you get angry is not a good idea, it's obviously destructive. This particular situation happened in Rama's presence for a special purpose.

"There is always a divine message hidden in the seemingly negative experiences we go through. We just have to penetrate beneath the surface of a situation, and the message will be revealed. But we usually remain on the outer surface of our experiences."

The car stopped at the entrance of the hall and Mother stepped out into the waiting crowd. As the people caught sight of Mother, spontaneous smiles lit up their faces. They were like lotus flowers blossoming at the mere appearance of the sun in the sky. A baby girl straddling her mother's hip was staring at Mother. Mother walked over to the baby and kissed her, calling, "Baby, baby!" The child broke into a smile and reached out for Mother, wanting to come to Her. Mother lifted the little girl into Her arms and walked towards the entrance of the hall, where She stopped for the traditional pada puja, garlanding, and arati. With the baby still in Her arms, Mother then proceeded to the stage.

<hr />

Charleston

Jivan mukti

In Charleston, Virginia, Mother gave darshan in a non-sectarian church. She had been invited there by a monk, who ran the place. He treated Mother with great reverence. Before the bhajans he told the gathering, "This may be the first time Mother comes to America—the first time She comes here in the body, that is...." Pausing for a moment he continued, "But I know that Mother has been here before. She has been with me. For She came to me in a vision, before I had ever heard of Her; and in that vision She told me that She was coming to America. Later I found out about Mother and that She was about to visit this country."

During the bhajans that followed Mother led everyone in the song, *Jay jay jay Durga Maharani.*

Victory, victory, victory to Durga,
The Great Queen!
O Durga, Great Queen,
Grant me Your vision!

O Enchantress of the universe,
O Mother who dwells in all the three worlds,
You are the One who gave birth to all of creation;
You are the Bestower of all boons;
O Durga, Great Queen,
Grant me Your vision!

O Mother Durga,
You are the One who destroys all ignorance,
You are the One who removes all fears and sorrows;
O Mother, who is seated on a lion,
You are the embodiment of all that is auspicious.
O Durga, Great Queen,
Grant me Your vision!

O Mother,
You are the embodiment of faith,
Compassion, and love;
You alone are the Great Illusion,
The Supreme Power;
O Mother Bhavani,
You dwell in all hearts.
O Durga, Great Queen,
Grant me Your vision!

Victory, victory, victory
To Durga, the Great Queen!

When the darshan began, a woman who had been traveling with Mother, came up to Her for darshan and then sat down next to Her. She had heard Mother talk about jivan mukti, and wanted to know more about the subject. She said, "Amma, the other day you were talking about the ultimate state of liberation, a state of freedom from all bondage to body and mind, which can be experienced while still living in this world. You said that in that state, the body and mind cease to exist. Does that mean that the world will disappear before our eyes? Because without the body and mind, how can one experience the world?"

Mother: "The state of jivan mukti doesn't mean that the world disappears. The world will continue to exist. But your wrong notions about the world will disappear. It is your wrong understanding that causes all differences and diversity. This will dissolve and you will behold only the oneness of everything, everywhere. But God's creation will still be there; for you can only destroy what you yourself have created. In other words, you can destroy the ego, for that is your own creation. This universe is not your creation, so you can't do anything about it.

"Your thoughts are your own creation. You make them real by cooperating with them. Withdraw your support and they will dissolve. Observe your thoughts. Don't love or hate them, don't judge them as good or bad. Just be an onlooker and they will disappear. The external world will not disappear just because you observe it. But if you can be a detached witness, the inner world of thoughts will disappear. Just imagine that the world of thoughts is a flowing river, and you are an observer standing on the bank of the river, without jumping into it.

"The clouds in the sky have different shapes. A cloud may take the form of a monster, a chariot, a prancing horse, or the beautiful face of a god—and as the cloud drifts by, it continues to change. Small children enjoy this. As they watch the passing clouds, they may believe the shapes are real. But a grownup knows that the shapes are illusions, that they are only clouds continuously changing their forms. The grownups don't judge; they just look at the sky without any attitude, without commenting on the shapes they see up there. They don't say: 'O, what a beautiful horse!' because they know it's only a cloud. In the same way, thoughts are the ever-changing 'clouds' that appear in the inner space of the mind. They may assume different shapes but they are always unreal. Because you haven't created the clouds in the external sky, they won't disappear as a result of your observing them. However, the clouds of thought in the inner sky will dissolve if you can simply witness them as they go by.

"A lion made of sandalwood is real to a child, but to a grownup it's a piece of sandalwood. For the child, the wood is concealed, revealing only the lion. The grownup may also enjoy the lion, but he knows it is not real. For him, the wood is real, and not the lion.

"In the same way, to a jivan mukta, the entire universe is nothing but the essence, the 'wood', that everything is made of, the Absolute Brahman or Consciousness.

"The world doesn't disappear before the jivan mukta's eyes. Everything continues as it is. Nothing changes. The sun doesn't stop rising on the western horizon when someone attains realization. However, a change happens inwardly. You perceive the world from a different level of consciousness. For the jivan mukta, everything is permeated with God, with pure, undivided Consciousness. Just as the wooden lion is still a piece of wood to a grownup, the jivan mukta beholds everything as the Paramatman, the Supreme Self. The world of names and forms still exists, but he perceives the inner essence of everything. Being in the state of jivan mukti doesn't mean that you lose your body. You can stay in your body and continue to function in the world, but your identification with the body has ceased. You become an observer, a witness. You stop experiencing the world from the outside. You observe everything from within, from the true center of existence.

"The kernel of a dry coconut automatically separates from the hard outer shell. The kernel remains inside the shell without being attached to it. It is the same with a jivan mukta, because, in that state, the soul and the body are seen to be separate. The delusion that the body is the soul, or that the soul is the body, is removed. All attachments to the body vanish. When the vasanas (latent tendencies) have 'dried up', the realization dawns on you that the body is not the Self, but that the Self is totally free and independent. To the jivan mukta, the Self is everything, everywhere—the Paramatman has become the entire creation.

"There is a beautiful story about Lord Brahma, the Creator of the universe. It is said that after creating each living being, the Lord fell in love with it to such an extent that He entered into His creation and became one with it. He created a tree, He fell in love with the tree and became the tree. He created a pig, He fell in love with the pig and became the pig. He created a human being, fell in love with the person and became that person. Thus he entered into everything.

"God has fallen in love with His creation. He permeates everything, as the one life-giving Power. Jivan mukti is the state in which you behold the glory of God, His infinite power, within everything—not only in what is good and beautiful, but also in all that is bad and ugly. You see the inner essence of the world, not the outer surface. The surface of things remains the same, but your inner eye has opened, allowing you to penetrate the exterior and to clearly perceive 'That' which lies within.

"In the *Srimad Bhagavatam*, Prahlada, a boy who worshipped Lord Vishnu, told his father, the demon king Hiranyakashipu, that the Lord is everywhere, whether it be in a blade of grass, an inert pillar, a dry leaf, a simple hut, or a palace. Hiranyakashipu, who was enraged at his son's faith in the Lord, pointed at a large pillar inside the palace and shouted at the boy, 'Is your Hari in that pillar too?' Without a moment's hesitation, the boy replied, 'Yes, He is there too.' The demon was infuriated by this and struck the pillar with his sword. The force of the blow split the pillar in two and out came the fierce form of Narasimha (the divine man-lion) in an explosion of Cosmic Power.

"Without the Supreme Energy nothing could exist. Without the integrating force of the Cosmic Power, which holds everything together, the world would dissolve in an instant. The Supreme Energy is the ultimate building force.

"The story symbolizes the all-pervasive, omnipresent nature of the Supreme Energy. Jivan mukti is the highest point of human existence, a state in which one constantly experiences eternal bliss while still in the body. In that state, the body is no more than a cage for the soul to dwell in, for you are always aware of the Self being different from the body.

"Have you heard of King Janaka, the father of Sita Devi who was the holy consort of Lord Rama? King Janaka was a jivan mukta. He was one with the Self; and yet he never turned his back on his responsibilities as a king. He ruled the land and did his duty with perfect equanimity. He remained completely untouched and detached from the events that took place in his life, whether they happened to be good or bad.

"In the state of jivan mukti, the world still exists, but one's whole perspective changes. Having attained oneness with the Supreme Being, the jivan mukta performs the duties entrusted to him for as long as he continues to live in the world. He doesn't sit idle saying, 'Everything is an illusion, so there's no reason for me to do any work?'"

❧❦

Boston

The avatar

This morning, a young man expressed a wish to ask Mother a question. Mother smiled at him and said, "Of course you can. But do not ask anything about God, karma (the theory of action), or moksha."

The man was bewildered; for how could he ask a spiritual question without touching on any of those subjects? Seeing his puzzled expression, Mother and the devotees laughed. Mother hugged him and said, "Son, don't worry. You can ask your question."

Although, Mother had been joking when She said he wasn't to mention anything about those three subjects, it was a deeply significant statement; because any question about God, karma, or moksha remains unanswerable. Nothing can be said about these subjects because, unless they are experienced directly, they cannot be understood. Any explanations or interpretations will only create more questions. Mother says, "Words will delude you. Go beyond words, and you will know." However, when a great master like Mother speaks to us, their words spring forth from their immediate experience of the highest Truth. So the words of a God-realized soul are the only reliable source we have on these subjects.

Having received permission to proceed with his question, the man asked, "Amma, are you an *avatar*? Are you the Divine Mother? Are you Adi Parashakti (the Supreme Power)?"

Mother: "You may call this body by any name you like. Some call it Amma (Mother), some Devi or Krishna, yet others consider it to be a Buddha or a Christ. There are many who call this body Amritanandamayi and other names. There are also those who criticize this body. It doesn't matter to Amma what you call Her. The Truth, the inner Self, remains eternally the same—immutable and unaffected. No one can pierce the mystery of this pure being.

"The word 'avatar' means to descend. The infinite Consciousness descends into the world, assuming a human form for the sake of uplifting and saving humanity. However, this is only from the standpoint of the devotee, because there is no space for the infinite Consciousness to come and go. Where could that which is infinite and all-pervasive possibly descend or ascend to? There's not an extra inch of space in which to move. Ascending and descending exist only for those who do not experience their oneness with the Supreme Reality. When you are one with the ocean of Sat-Chit-Ananda, there is no question of coming or going.

"One could say that when a soul attains realization, the clay pot in the ocean breaks, and the water inside the pot merges with the water that surrounds it, so that there is nothing but water everywhere. Here the ocean represents the infinite Consciousness or the Paramatman, and the clay pot is the individual Self. In the ultimate state of realization, your individuality or body-consciousness disappears. You merge with the Infinite and go beyond all limitations. For an avatar, however, there was never a clay pot to break, for he or she has always been one with the Supreme.

"The avatars live among human beings, undergoing all the hardships of life; but they are constantly setting an example of divine love, compassion, self-sacrifice, etc. Such beings become a great source of inspiration for millions of people all over the globe. They are like great ships that can carry hundreds of thousands of people across the ocean of transmigration. The avatars are born with perfect awareness of the Supreme Truth. They may perform severe austerities, but they do so only to set an example for the world. It is like a loving mother whose child is suffering from jaundice and has to follow a strict diet. To make it easier for her child, she will follow the same diet. For if she eats any other food in front of her child, he may feel tempted to do the same.

"If you wish to communicate with someone who is deaf and dumb, you cannot speak to them in your own language. To get the message across, you have to communicate in sign language. You have to go to their level. But though you are using sign language, it doesn't mean that you yourself are deaf. Likewise, the avatars may undergo severe austerities, or you may see them meditating, but that doesn't mean that they really need to do so. Whatever spiritual practices they do are done to set an example to others and thereby inspire and uplift them.

"Everything in nature moves in an endless circle: there is birth, death, and again, birth. The seasons move in a circle: spring, summer, autumn, winter, and spring again. The earth moves on its axis around the sun. A seed germinates and becomes a tree; the tree blossoms, and new seeds are born. The ages (yugas) also move in a circle: there is the *Satya yuga, Treta yuga, Dwapara yuga, Kali yuga,* and again the Satya yuga. Before this creation there was another creation. This universe will eventually cease to exist, and another universe will manifest. When Rama descended to the world, he said to Hanuman: 'There have been countless Rama avatars, not just this one.' And Krishna said to Arjuna, 'You and I have been born together a number of times. I know all about it, but you do not.'"

Amritatma exclaimed, "O Amma, I remember you said once that all those who are with you now have been with you before."

Mother: "Yes, all of Amma's children who are with Amma now have been with Her before."

A clear sign

The question about Mother being Adi Parashakti, the Supreme Power, brings an incident to mind.

A young man, Madhavan, who was a student of *Tantra* and worshipped the Divine Mother in the form of Sri Lalita Parameshvari, came to see Mother for the first time. He was standing at the bottom of Mother's staircase, waiting for Her to come down from Her room. As he was waiting, he thought, "If Mother really is Sri Lalitambika (an aspect of the Divine Mother as Sri Lalita), who is *Karpūra vīṭikāmoda samākarṣi digantarā*[12] (She who enjoys camphor-laden betel rolls, the fragrance of which attracts the entire creation),[13] She has to give me a sign so that I will know."

A few minutes later Mother came down the stairs. He noticed that She was chewing something. (Mother doesn't normally walk around chewing anything.)

When She reached the bottom of the stairs where Madhavan was standing, She opened Her mouth and, pointing at it, said, "Look, son! This is *karpūra vitikā*. A devotee gave it to Amma."

Madhavan was speechless. He couldn't have asked for a clearer sign. It turned out that one of Mother's devotees from a nearby town called Kottayam, who was always chanting the *Sri Lalitā Sahasranāma*, and who strongly believed that Mother was none other than Adi Parashakti, had given Mother the karpūra vitikā

---

[12] One of the names of the Divine Mother in the Sri Lalitasahasranama.

[13] Karpura Vitika is a combination of cardamom, coconut, black pepper, ginger, and lime.

as an offering a few days earlier. But Mother hadn't touched it because She normally doesn't chew such things. However, that particular day, before She left Her room, Mother took a pinch of the substance which had been kept on a table, and put it in Her mouth. It became clear to Madhavan that Mother knew his every thought, and that She was none other than Devi Herself.

As the darshan continued, another question was asked: "Amma, you mentioned that there have been countless Rama and Krishna avatars. But we have heard of only one Rama and one Krishna. What, then, do you mean by this?"

Mother: "Even today, Rama, Krishna, and Buddha could come back, and it is happening—but people don't have eyes to see. Don't look for Rama or Krishna in the same forms as before. If you look for Rama with a bow and arrow, or Krishna with a flute and a peacock feather, you are bound to be disappointed. God is not a miser; He spends lavishly. His extravagance appears before humanity in many forms. Rama, Krishna, and Buddha are appearing in different forms. No, you won't find them in this world if you expect them to have exactly the same bodies as before, or to dress in the same way as they once did, or if you expect their play on earth to be the same as it once was. No, they will not be exactly the same. However, if you really long to see them, it is possible to find them. Search for them where there is divine love, where everyone is loved equally and unconditionally and there is boundless compassion; where there is great humility and self-sacrifice. Wherever you come across those qualities, that is where Rama and Krishna dwell.

"God is infinite. He once appeared as Rama and Krishna. That all-pervasive, limitless Consciousness, with its inexhaustible energy, is now assuming another form.

(Jokingly) "People get bored with everything, don't they? They may even get bored with God if He were to come again as

Rama or Krishna. Because God knows how easily humans get bored, He wishes to amuse everyone with His infinite wisdom, and so He appears in different forms!"

"Children, the container changes but the content remains the same—that doesn't change. This is what happens with an avatar. Also, each divine incarnation appears according to the needs of society at the time. The problems of the world today, the solutions to those problems, and the ways to implement those solutions are different from what they were during Rama's and Krishna's time."

Br. Amritatma, who was translating Mother's words, was reminded of how a few months earlier, at the ashram in India, Mother had incidentally referred to Herself in the middle of a conversation, saying: "The saints and sages performed years of severe tapas to realize God. Here you have God right in your midst—but how many people care?"

≈≫≪≈

New York

"I am your Mother"

During the first morning program in New York, when Mother had just begun giving darshan, She pointed at a little blond boy, who was sitting with his father at the other side of the room, and said to Amritatma, "That child has no mother. Amma feels great love and compassion for him." The boy had not been up to Mother yet, and no one had told Her anything about him.

After a while, Mother playfully tossed a chocolate kiss across the room to where the little boy was sitting. He smiled and ate the chocolate. Soon after, Mother threw another chocolate halfway across the room. He walked a little closer to Mother and got his second treat. Mother repeated this a few more times and when he was close enough, Mother reached out and grabbed him. They both laughed. The little boy immediately felt a strong bond with Mother.

His father, Larry Richmond (Arun), came up to Mother and explained that his son, Jason, who was six years old, had lost his mother when he was only eight months old; that he often woke up crying at night, asking why he didn't have a mother. Mother held Jason in Her arms and said to him, "Jason, I am your Mother!" Jason gazed at Mother in wonder. He thought Mother meant that She was his biological mother. His face shone with joy. For the first time in his life he was experiencing the unconditional love of a mother.

Larry also told Mother that Jason suffered from epilepsy; that he had frequent seizures and the medication didn't help at all. Mother told Larry to continue giving him the medication. She gave him a piece of sandalwood and instructed him on how to use it.

Mother's instructions were followed to the letter, and from then on, Jason never had another seizure.

The humility of a Satguru

During an evening program at the Cathedral of St. John the Divine in New York, Mother was asked a question.

"Amma, in California I heard you talk about the humility of a true master; that a satguru doesn't have any sense of ego and that he bows down to all of creation. My question is whether humility is an integral part of a Self-realized master."

Mother: "A Self-realized master is beyond everything. But humility will be one of the basic qualities that he or she expresses. The master is humble because he perceives everything as God and worships the entire creation as the Supreme. So you could say that a satguru is always in a worshipful, prayerful mood. He bows down to everything, and all of existence, in turn, bows down to him.

"No inner change is possible around an egoistic person. The sadhak (aspirant) cannot be transformed if the feeling of 'I' and 'mine' are predominant in the master. Such so-called teachers can only create fear and anxiety around them, which closes all possibilities of transformation.

"There have been many cruel kings and dictators all over the world, who have cared only about their own interests and nothing else. During their reign, terror prevailed and people's hearts were consequently closed. But there have also been many examples of great souls who have changed the lives of countless people for the better, with nothing more than their humble presence. Every trace of fear disappears in the proximity of such beings. A genuine master is beyond all egoism. True humility creates a vibration of love and compassion which, in turn, produces the necessary conditions for a spiritual unfoldment to take place. This is why the presence of a satguru provides the most suitable atmosphere in which your heart can blossom.

"A Self-realized master dwells eternally in the Self, unperturbed by the different experiences of life. You may observe that the master is humbler than the humblest, simpler than the simplest, inconceivably loving, compassionate, and patient—and yet, he is none of these, for he is beyond all qualities. His mastery over the mind and the senses gives him the unlimited capacity to focus on any divine quality, and to manifest that quality, fully and perfectly, expressing it in any way he chooses. But the next moment he can withdraw from it, totally untouched and detached.

"Though a master may be humble for the sake of setting an example, it is impossible to judge him as being this or that. Of course he is humble but, at the same time, he is beyond that.

"A disciple should learn to be humble, for it is through humility that true discipleship is born. Unless this quality is awakened, the master cannot really enter into your life.

"It is this awakening of the disciple within you that brings the master to you. Your intense thirst to know the Truth gives birth to the disciple within. The lover within you awakens, and once the lover is awakened, the beloved appears. Without the lover, there is no beloved; without the disciple, there is no master—the master will still exist, but not in your life.

"The disciple's humility—his attitude of being an absolute beginner, and his acceptance and awareness of his own ignorance—makes him open and receptive to true knowledge, which the master then pours into him. Humility is the gateway to real discipleship, and the master will himself set a perfect example of humility.

"Without the slightest hesitation, Sri Rama touched the feet of his stepmother, Kaikeyi, and sought her blessing before he left to spend fourteen years of exile in the forest—even though it was Kaikeyi who was responsible for his exile. Rama was humble enough to lovingly and respectfully bow down to her, without a thought of anger or revenge.

"Look at the example of Sri Krishna's life. He was perfectly aware of His divinity, of who He was. Yet He humbly washed the feet of all the saints and sages who came to participate in the *rajasuya*, which was being performed by Yudhisthira, the eldest of the Pandava brothers. Also, think of how, just before Lord Krishna left his mortal frame, He bestowed the state of moksha (liberation) on the hunter who was instrumental in putting an end to His life on earth. Amma has also heard that the night before his crucifixion, Christ washed and kissed the feet of all his apostles, including Judas, who betrayed him for thirty silver coins."

There is an Amma hidden within everyone

Question: "Amma, by their selflessness and the example of their lives, those great souls have inspired and uplifted humanity. But is there any 'inner' significance to their great deeds?"

Mother: "Every human being, even if he or she happens to be cruel and selfish, has the capacity to become enlightened. This capacity lies dormant in everyone. Amma sees an Amma hidden in each one of you. There is a Krishna, Rama, Buddha, or Christ within you. God's divine light could dawn within you at any moment; it's just waiting for the right opportunity to arise. The great masters are able to see that hidden light which is waiting to emerge, waiting to break through the walls of the ego. They behold a future Krishna, Rama, Buddha, or Christ within everyone. Seeing the Divine Mother within you, Amma bows down to Her own Self—to God. This is what the great masters have always done. The masters can clearly see the Divinity within you, but you yourself cannot perceive it because of your lack of awareness. The masters can see the Divine Light within you, which is why they bow down to it. You cannot be truly humble unless you are able to perceive this light in everyone. It is the experience of the Self that makes you naturally humble in all situations. When you behold everything as God, you are always in a worshipful mood. When there are no feelings of otherness, your whole life becomes an act of worship, a form of prayer, a song of praise. The 'other' disappears, and in its place you behold the dormant state of enlightenment, the innermost Self, in the person standing before you. You then feel a deep sense of reverence towards that person. In that state, nothing is insignificant for you; everything has its special place. You behold the Supreme Light shining even in a blade of grass."

Mother Herself is the living embodiment of every word She preaches. Mother prostrates before everyone when She is about

137

to give darshan, and again when the darshan is over. She accepts any offering a devotee may give Her, bowing down to it with reverence and gratitude, whether it is something very significant, or a fruit or just a simple leaf.

Who has not seen Mother worship Her children at the end of Devi Bhava, showering flower petals on them? Who hasn't heard about the incident when Mother visited the man who had tried to kill Her, when he lay dying in the hospital, and how She lovingly fed him with Her own hands?

Thousands of people have witnessed Mother treating Dattan the leper with Her healing saliva; and in the early days, at the end of each Devi Bhava, the devotees would line up around the little temple, and then Mother would dance around the temple three times, touching and blessing the people as She passed them. Dattan would be waiting for Mother behind the temple with two pitchers of water. When Mother came around the temple the third time, She would pause in front of Dattan and pour the water over him, giving him a bath.

One year, when Mother was staying in Seattle, She returned to the house at about 3:30 one morning, after having given darshan for many hours. As Mother walked along the garden path towards the door, She suddenly jumped back saying that She had trodden on something. She bent down and found a snail that She had touched with Her foot, and which was slightly injured. "Oh no!" She exclaimed. "Poor thing!" She picked it up and held it in Her cupped hands. Looking sadly at the little snail, She said, "This poor creature's mate will be looking for him soon. She will be very worried, wondering what has happened to him." Mother continued to gaze at the snail in Her hands for several minutes. She then closed Her eyes, held the snail to Her forehead, and then gently put it down beneath a plant before She went into the house.

Though Mother is one with God, She worships every being in creation as a manifestation of God. What greater examples could one possibly need to be inspired?

❧❧

Stamford, Connecticut

The last program in the US was held in a small house near Stamford in Connecticut. Mother gave darshan sitting on an upside-down milk cart with an asana spread on top of it.

In the late afternoon Mother meditated with the devotees beside a lake. Everyone was disturbed and was having trouble sitting still because the air was thick with swarms of biting mosquitoes. Only Mother was unaffected. Surrounded by a cloud of mosquitoes, She sat perfectly still, in a completely absorbed mood, Her face glowing with serenity.

Amma is always with you

Mother's first American tour was drawing to a close. The evening before Mother left the States, She turned to a young woman at the house where She was staying and asked, "Why are you so sad?"

"Because Amma is going," said the women.

"Where!" was Mother's immediate response.

From Connecticut, Mother was driven to JFK airport in New York, where a group of devotees were waiting to bid Her a tearful farewell. Before going through the passport control, Mother tenderly took each one of them in Her arms.

She said to them: "Children, Amma is always with you. Each time you think of Her, Amma can clearly see your faces. And do you know," She continued, "at the ashram in India, every night when Amma lies down to rest, Amma goes out to all Her children all over the world. Amma's children are Her swans, and like a shepherd Amma checks on them and brings any straying swan back into Her fold. You are all baby birds, and Amma is keeping you under Her wing."

As Mother was about to leave through the passport control, several in the group shouted, "Mother, please come back to us!" Mother looked at them with great affection and said, "Don't worry, children. Amma will come back." She saluted them with Her folded hands above Her head, and said softly in English: "My children...."

Thus, having sown the seeds of true spirituality in the soil of the United States of America, and in the hearts of those who had come to see Her, Mother left for Europe on July 14. But Her subtle presence was to remain with Her children.

Within a short period of time, Mother had brought about a great transformation in people; their whole outlook on life had changed. Without giving scholarly lectures, or talks delivered with flowery words; but rather, by Her simple, innocent approach—reaching out to everyone through Her all-embracing love, Her mere presence, touch and look—Mother became permanently established in people's hearts. Though She spoke in Her mother-tongue, Malayalam, language or nationality was not a barrier in any way. Enfolded in Her loving arms, people spontaneously poured out their hearts to Her. They simply opened up. And they realized that a divine message was being imparted to them through Mother's every movement. Her eyes and Her smile spoke to them. Her every breath seemed to convey something divine. Her whole being silently communicated with them. Y

Europe

Mother arrived in Paris in the early morning of July 15, 1987. Sarvatma (Jacques Albohair) and a few other devotees welcomed Mother at the airport. When the devotees saw Mother coming towards them, they just stood there stared at Her in wonderment. They knew nothing about the Indian custom of garlanding the guru; they just gazed innocently at Mother, not knowing what to do. Mother greeted them with great warmth, like long lost children. While She waited for the luggage to pass through customs, She sat down on the floor in a corner of the airport and hugged everyone. She asked each person simple questions about their health, where they lived, and so on. She came down to their level and talked to them in this way just to break the ice and to make them feel more familiar with Her.

When the luggage had been organized, the devotees drove everyone to Kathy and Daniel Demilly's house in Dourdan outside Paris. There were a few people waiting for Mother at the house. Mother embraced them, talked to them for a while, and then retired to Her room to rest.

The first darshan took place in the living room later that afternoon. About forty people attended. Mother sat on the floor and called the devotees one by one. She spent five to ten minutes with each person, holding them, caressing them, putting sacred ash on their foreheads, giving each person a sweet, speaking to them and asking questions. Many of the people, both men and women, young and old, shed tears in Mother's presence. They were deeply moved; for it was clear to them that Mother knew everything about them, every detail of their lives, their past and their future, and every thought in their minds; and yet, in Her there was not a trace of judgment, only a boundless, unconditional love that was unmistakable—a love greater than any love they had ever encountered. Each person was made to feel that he or she was Mother's most precious child.

In the late afternoon, Mother went to Her room, and there She continued to see the people who had come up to Her earlier and had expressed a wish to talk to Her in private.

As in the U.S., almost all the morning programs in Europe took place in people's homes, while the evening programs were held in different halls.

～～

Paris

Facing problems

In Paris a devotee told Mother about his strong desire to leave his job because of the stressful situations he was experiencing there. He said, "Amma, I feel helpless and confused whenever I have to deal with so much stress. What do you suggest that I should do?"

Mother: "Whenever you are confronted with a difficult situation, your first instinct is to escape, to somehow avoid it and run away. People think that by doing so, they can get rid of their problems. But this is not so. They may be able to escape for a while, but sooner or later the same difficulties will reappear with even greater force than before.

"It should be understood that external situations don't have the power to hurt you. It is only when the mind interprets those situations that the pain bubbles up from within. A situation becomes a problem when you interpret it in the wrong way. The aim is to not let the mind interpret or comment on external situations. This is possible only when you learn the art of witnessing.

"Children, your problems do not lie in the outer circumstances. You cannot avoid external situations. They are part of life. For example, one fine morning, an elderly woman walks into the home of a married couple. The husband sees her and rejoices. 'O Mother, how wonderful to see you!' he exclaims. But his wife doesn't have a pleasant look on her face at all when she sees her mother-in-law. How do you explain this? How can the same person create such widely different reactions in two people? She didn't do anything except walk through the door! It was simply a situation. But for one person it became a joyous moment, while for the other it was a cause for great unhappiness. For one person it was a problem, while for the other it was the opposite. So the aim is to not let the mind interpret or comment on external situations. But our minds are so weak and judgmental that we naturally fall victim to situations and become deluded. The problem arises when you react negatively to those situations. In other words, the root of your troubles exist within yourself. Straighten out the creases of the mind, where the problems really exist, and the external creases will automatically disappear.

"Some students come and say, 'Amma, my exam paper was a terrible problem.' Amma asks them, 'Where is the problem? Is it to be found in the question paper? No, because there are others who have succeeded very well in the same exam. The real difficulty is you yourself, because you didn't study hard enough. So it may have been a problem for you, but it wasn't a problem for those who really applied themselves and studied the subject.'

"Many people tell Amma that they have difficulties with their husband or wife. But the same husband or wife is often a good friend to someone else, a brother or sister to someone, and a loving parent to their children. To the Pandavas, Krishna was a good friend, whereas the Kauravas thought of him as their enemy. Similarly, the believers looked upon Jesus as their beloved friend and savior, whereas others saw him as a threat. Would you say that the problem lay with Krishna or Jesus? No, the problem lay with the Kauravas and with those who doubted Jesus.

"In the West people date for a long time, and then, if they like each other they get married and have children. They are happy for some time, but soon difficulties arise. Conflicts based on fear and anger begin to manifest. They both want to escape the situation and run away, and so they end up separating. After their divorce, they may live on sweet and painful memories for a while; but it won't be long before they begin dating someone else, and they'll again go through the same cycle of experiences. Think of how often this happens. People keep abusing each other, and criticizing each other's faults and weaknesses. They are not aware of the fact that the problems exist within themselves.

"You may run away from that person now; you may run from one marriage to another, hoping that your troubles have been put behind you at last—but it won't be long before you find the same person, that is, someone with the same weaknesses and the same level of consciousness, in another 'wrapper' and in a different situation. You may find it even worse than before. The outer appearance of the person has changed, but the content—the level of consciousness within that 'wrapper'—remains the same. This is because you haven't changed. So the level of consciousness of the partners you choose is the same as before. Only the outer appearances differ.

"Unless there is a considerable shift in your consciousness, and thus in your attitude, your problems won't go away. They will continue to appear everywhere, constantly disturbing you. Your mind will continue to persuade you to escape from the situations of life, deluding you with false promises about the future.

"By changing a very common misconception—the idea that your problems are to be found in the outer situations of life—you can remove your problems once and for all. Understand that the difficulties are to be found within your own mind. Once you become aware of this, you can begin the process of removing your inner weaknesses. Meditation is the method that is used to achieve this. Only the inner silence, stillness, and relaxation which you gain through meditation will help."

At Mother's request, the brahmacharis then sang a song called *Shakti Mahadevi.*

Salutations to Shakti, the Great Goddess
Who can be reached through devotion
Salutations to the Seed
The One Truth
Infinite and Perfect Awareness

O my Divine Lotus
Left eye of Shiva
Fulfiller of all desires
Ruler of all
Who shines through everything
Protect me

You are the Goddess of the celestials
Protecting them from all sorrows
You are the Pure One
Who protects even the Lord of the Ocean of Milk

The Creator does his work
Only because of Your glance
Salutations to You who came forth out of Brahma
As Saraswati
The Seed of the entire Universe

Creation, sustenance, and destruction
Take place at Your command

145

O Destroyer of the eight-faceted ego
Who is fond of the sound of the veena
When angered
You are also fond of blood

You are the Veda
The Absolute
You are in all living beings
You are the ultimate liberation

Optimism

During darshan one evening, a woman came up to Mother and told Her that almost all her hopes about life had vanished. Mother said, "My daughter, as long as you are able to trust in God, there is no need to give up. Sometimes you may feel that all the doors are closed to you, that there is no way out; but if you look carefully, you will see that there are still many doors that are wide open. You are focusing only on the closed doors and thus you miss the ones that are open to you.

"Life and God are one and the same. You are God's child. God would never close all the doors around you. His unlimited love and compassion wouldn't allow Him to be that cruel. God always keeps more than one door open. They may look as if they are closed, but they have, in fact, been left slightly ajar. Just a mild knock is enough and they'll give way. But our eyes are blinded by our ignorance. We fail to see the open doors through which the light of God's grace is pouring in.

"My child, never lose courage. Never lose your trust in God or in life. Always be optimistic, no matter what situations you find yourself in. It's very important to be optimistic. Pessimism is a form of darkness, a form of ignorance that prevents God's light from entering into your life. Pessimism is like a curse, an illusory curse created by the illusory mind. Life is filled with God's light, but only by being optimistic will you experience that light.

"Look at the optimism of nature. Nothing can stop it. Every aspect of nature tirelessly contributes its share to life. The participation of a little bird, an animal, a tree, or a flower is always complete. No matter what the hardships, they continue to try, wholeheartedly. Only humans are pessimistic, and this causes suffering.

"Amma has heard a story. A shoe company sent two sales representatives to a distant island, where only primitives lived. Their mission was to explore the sales opportunities on the island. Some time later, one of the salesmen sent a message to the company, 'The people here don't even know what shoes are! They don't wear shoes! The situation is hopeless. I'm coming back.' This was followed by a message from his partner: 'These primitives don't wear shoes. They don't know anything about them. Plenty of opportunity—100% chance! Send me the first shipment.'

"Amma knows it isn't easy to always be optimistic. You may ask, how is it possible to be optimistic in the face of the many hardships and sorrows in life? It is true that it's difficult—but by being pessimistic you move towards even greater despair and darkness. All your strength and clarity of mind gets dissipated; and in the darkness of pessimism you feel abandoned and isolated. Optimism is the light of God. It is a form of grace which allows you to be much more perceptive and to look at life with greater clarity."

Patience and enthusiasm

A woman who had been on the spiritual path for a long time said to Mother, "Amma, I have practiced meditation since 1973, but even so, I haven't experienced any progress. At times I feel so disappointed that I stop doing my sadhana. Could you please advise me?"

Mother smiled and asked, "No progress at all?"

The woman replied, "Well…actually, there has been some progress."

"How much progress? Can you say something about it?" Mother asked.

"I'll try." The woman thought for a moment. "I used to be very sensitive and felt extremely vulnerable. But since I began meditating and doing other spiritual practices, I think I've gained more courage and self-confidence."

"You *think*. Daughter, that means you're not very sure."

The woman was perplexed. She said, "Amma, you're like an investigating officer!"

Mother laughed and retorted, "Yes, Amma explores and investigates your inner self. She tries to pull out the old in order to create the new."

Mother gazed lovingly at the woman. She put Her arms around her and hugged her affectionately.

"My daughter, a spiritual seeker must have a lot of patience and enthusiasm. There are some who are patient but not enthusiastic; others are enthusiastic but lack patience. Only a perfect balance between the two will help a seeker to deepen his experience.

"Look at the youngsters. They are very enthusiastic about doing things but they don't have the patience to think things through. It is patience that opens up the gateway to discriminative thinking. The youngsters, however, in their one-sided enthusiasm, tend to jump into things, without giving anything the necessary thought. Their senses are strong and healthy, and their egoistic minds are drawn to thrills and adventure; but their lack of patience and discrimination often land them in trouble.

"On the other hand, elderly people in their sixties or seventies are usually very patient, but they lack enthusiasm. Experience has taught them to be patient, to do things with more discrimination. They are therefore far more thoughtful. But they don't have the necessary enthusiasm to do things. They cannot be as enthusiastic as teenagers because their senses have weakened, their strength has deteriorated, and they have lost the thrill of life.

"Look at a toddler who is trying to stand up and walk. The child will fall countless times, failing in his every attempt. He may bruise his knee, hit his head on the floor, and cry; but, again and again, he will stubbornly try to get up and walk, until he finally succeeds. Though the child fails, not once but countless times, he is both patient and enthusiastic. These qualities finally help the child to succeed in his attempts.

"Another notable point is the constant encouragement the child receives from its mother. Fortunately for the child, the mother is always there with supportive words, providing the child with faith and courage. Whenever the toddler falls, the mother's loving hands are there to pick him up. She kisses and caresses him saying, 'Don't cry. It's all right. Mother is here.' She puts the child down and persuades him to try again. This happens innumerable times before the infant is finally able to stand on his own feet and walk with steady steps.

"The mother's encouraging words and soothing touch helps the child to develop. Her love gives the child the inner strength it needs. In the same way, a sadhak needs the patience and enthusiasm of a child—but most importantly, he needs the loving presence and encouragement of a satguru to guide him to the goal. It is the master's presence that encourages the sadhak to be patient, enthusiastic, and optimistic during times of frustration and lack of hope, when he feels like giving up his sadhana.

"Children, your vasanas are extremely strong and deep-rooted. They will try to pull you down, again and again. But don't ever give up hope. Be determined and proceed.

"Suppose a person has been sitting in a dark room for a long time. Then one day he comes out into the sunlight. To begin with, he will find it difficult to get used to the light. It will take time for his eyes to adjust. Similarly, we have been living in this world believing that we are the body. We have become so identified with it that, now, as we try to withdraw that identification, we find it very difficult. We have become so accustomed to the darkness of our ignorance that we find it hard to come out into the light of God.

"The strength of our vasanas and age-old habits are such that we cannot easily free ourselves from their grip. As soon as the situation arises, the vasanas automatically manifest. Amma will tell you a story.

"There were two children, a brother and a sister. One day they dressed up in robes and put paper crowns on their heads. They pretended they were the king and queen of the land. They walked over to the neighbor's house and knocked on the door. 'Who is it?' she asked. 'It is the king and the queen,' said the children. The neighbor decided to play along with them. She opened the door wide and said, 'Your Majesties! What a great honor! Had I known you were coming, I would have laid out the red carpet and called the trumpeters.' 'It doesn't matter,' said the children. 'Just let us in and give us something to eat.' The woman led them inside and pulled out two chairs for them. 'Please sit on your thrones, your Majesties,' she said. The 'king' and 'queen' sat down with great dignity. The woman brought them homemade cookies and milk. 'Here are some delicacies fit for royalty,' she said. The king and queen nodded their approval. The cookies were beautiful, shaped like different animals. There was a large variety of bears, cats, fish, ducks, and lambs, but there was only one elephant cookie. And because there was only one elephant cookie, both the king and the queen wanted it. They both reached for it, but the queen got hold of it first. This made the king so angry that he threw his milk all over the queen. The queen grabbed a handful of cookies and threw them on the king. Soon they were bombarding each other with cookies, and then they jumped up from their thrones and began fighting in earnest. Their crowns flew off and their robes were torn. No more were they the king and queen of the land, but only two children fighting over a cookie.

"Only constant practice done with great patience and enthusiasm will enable you to overcome your latent tendencies and old habits. But above all, you need the grace and loving guidance of a satguru. Don't ever give up your spiritual practices just because of a moment's frustration or disappointment. Whatever type of sadhana you do, the result cannot be lost. Whatever you have gained remains within you and will bear fruit at the right time."

Mother closed Her eyes and became absorbed in a state of meditation. After some time, She opened Her eyes again and began to sing the song, *Karunalaye Devi.*

> *O Goddess*
> *Abode of Compassion*
> *Giver of all that we desire*
> *O Katyayani, Gauri, Sambhavi, Sankari!*[14]

> *Dearest Mother,*
> *Essence of Aum,*
> *You adore the Sound Aum*
> *O Mother, when You hear the mantra, "Om Shakti"*
> *You will come running!*
> *O Great Power of universal illusion.*

---

[14] Names of the Divine Mother

You are the Cause of the creation,
Preservation and destruction of the universe
O Mother, everything is You
You are everything
There is none other than You
O Mother, this suppliant has no support
Other than You, the Self of all Bliss
O Blissful Self, grant me a wonderful boon

Zurich

Here and now

In Zurich Mother stayed with Heidi Fürer. The first evening program was held in her house. Heidi had visited Mother at the ashram in India in 1984.

Although it was summer, the weather was cold in Zurich. The brahmacharis and the Indian householder devotees who were traveling with the group were not used to the cold. They wore sweaters and caps, but that didn't help them much. They froze so much that they had a difficult time getting out of their sleeping bags in the mornings.

During the first evening program a young man asked Mother a question.

"Most spiritual masters tell their disciples to forget about the past and future, and to live in the present moment. They teach many different techniques to help people attain this moment-by-moment living. Unfortunately, most of us are glued to the past and are worrying endlessly about the future. How is it possible for ordinary people, who are worried about how to pay their bills, their insurance, rent or house-payments, and their children's education, to stop being concerned about all the basic needs of life and, at the same time, to feel completely at peace? Isn't it the anxiety about the future that drives a person to work, earn money, and take proper care of his needs and obligations? Isn't it his past experiences that prompt him to be careful in the future, and to make sure that his mistakes are not repeated? Under these circumstances, how would it be possible for someone to live in the present moment, completely forgetting the past and the future?"

Mother: "What you have said about the concerns of most people is correct. No one can deny the reality of an ordinary individual's day-to-day worries. Past experiences certainly help a person to mold his future. It is also true that his dreams about the future inspire him to work and to fulfill those dreams. The real question, however, is whether there is any benefit to be had in regretting the past or being anxious about the future. You can plan your future on the basis of the experiences you have had and the lessons you have learnt from the past, but you don't have to dwell in the past or the future.

"You can plan your dinner, but not while preparing your lunch. Don't think about how much salt you will use in tonight's meal while adding salt to the soup you are cooking now. And don't regret that the soup you made yesterday wasn't a success. Just concentrate on the soup that is boiling on the stove at this moment. You want it to be healthy and delicious, don't you? So be alert and conscious of this moment.

"This teaching of living in the present moment can be viewed from two different angles: from that of the ordinary person who has professional, social, and family responsibilities; and from the standpoint of the sadhak who wants nothing but God-realization.

"For an ordinary person, who has worldly responsibilities to take care of, to completely forget the past and the future isn't possible, and he doesn't have to do that. Yet even for such a person, too much interference from the past and the future will prevent him from carrying out his duties properly in the present. An action always takes place in the present moment. To be able to carry it out properly, using all your talents and capabilities, you have to concentrate one hundred percent on the work at hand. Brooding or dreaming about something else will interfere with the work. Before you begin the work, you should think about any past related mistakes or failures, and prepare the mind for the job you are about to do. All calculations should be done beforehand. However, once the work has begun, all your attention should be on what you are doing now. In between, if you need to remember something, pause, go to the repository of the past, and find what you need to know. Then come out of there and continue with what you were doing, putting all your heart and soul into it. But do not stay with your memories, with your past. To be able to express yourself fully, you have to be present in the moment. Take, for example, a painter who is trying to capture the beauty of a landscape. If he thinks about his girlfriend while painting, he will do a mediocre job because his heart isn't in it. His focus is divided.

"A woman was on her way to the market carrying a basket of eggs on her head. As she walked along the road she began to daydream: 'I'll get a good price for these eggs. With the money I can buy a few more hens. Those hens will lay so many eggs that I'll soon be able to buy a cow. That cow will produce so much milk that before long I can afford to buy several cows. From the money I get from all that milk I shall buy a farm. The farm will make me so rich that I'll be able to buy a beautiful mansion. By then I'll be so rich that many young men will be after me. When I meet them on the street, I'll wiggle my hips and walk like this...'

And as the woman wiggled her hips, the basket fell from her head and all the eggs lay broken on the ground.

"Human beings have a deep tendency to dream about the future, to sail away on the wings of the imagination. Dreams belong to the future. Dreaming can make you inactive and incompetent. Dreaming needs no effort; if you have nothing else to do, you can simply sit down and dream about going to the moon, marrying a beautiful princess, or beating your opponent. It is the nature of the mind to brood over the past and to dream about tomorrow. Even a normally successful, active person can easily be caught in the clutches of the past and the future. People don't know how much energy they are wasting by immersing themselves in such thoughts. It is a great mistake if you keep thinking about the past or the future while engaged in some activity. You may be very talented and successful at what you do, but when you engage in such reverie you are killing half your talents, instead of utilizing your full capacity. In order to function fully, to be complete and perfect in your actions, you have to learn to live in the present moment. Then your total capacity will be channeled into whatever you do.

"Those who desire nothing but God-realization do not bother about the past or the future. Their wish is to be in the present moment, for that is where God is; that is where perfect peace and bliss is to be found. It is by being in this moment that you attain perfect stillness and quietude within. The past and the future are movements of the mind. The mind moves from the past to the future and back again, like the movement of a pendulum from one end to the other. The real center of existence is experienced when the pendulum of the mind reaches a point of stillness. The mind attains a state of stillness when it rests in the present moment. That stillness, or center, is what a true seeker yearns for, and this is why he doesn't bother about the past or the future. His focus is on the here and now. That is what is known as remembrance of God. Remembrance of God can only take place when you let go of the past and stop dreaming about the future. Then the pendulum of the mind stops swinging back and forth; it reaches a point of stillness, and you dwell in the stillness of the present moment."

Schweibenalp

Mother spent nine days in Schweibenalp in the Swiss Alps. People had come there from all over Europe to see Mother. A lot a families came and there were many children present. The small hall that had been prepared for Mother's darshan was jam-packed with people. They were joyful and enthusiastic, many of them dancing and singing in Mother's presence as if they were in seventh heaven. Because people had come from all over Europe, Mother's satsangs were translated into English, German, and French.

It was even colder in the Alps than it had been in Zurich. The brahmacharis and Indian devotees were walking around with clattering teeth, wearing woolen caps and several layers of thick clothes.

Miracles

During the first morning darshan a few questions were asked.

"Amma, could you say something about miracles? What exactly is a miracle?"

Mother: "Miracles are usually attributed to godmen. There is a widespread belief that only a divine being can perform a miracle, and that miracles are part and parcel of such a soul. People even believe that if a person doesn't perform any miracles, he cannot be a great soul, even though he may, in fact, be Self-realized. But our idea of what constitutes a miracle may or may not occur in the presence of the truly great ones, because they don't really care that much about such things. They have nothing to gain or lose by performing miracles. They don't care about name or fame, nor do they wish to please or displease anyone. If it happens, that's fine, and if it doesn't happen, that is also fine. Today, however, people's faith in God has come to depend on the miracles of a Self-realized master or a godman. Unfortunately, there are also so-called gurus whose only intention is to exploit and control people, and who like to draw attention to themselves by performing all sorts of miracles in public.

"To have absolute mastery over the mind is the same as having mastery over the universe. Everything in creation is made of the five elements: fire, water, earth, air, and ether. Once you attain God-realization, all the elements are under your control. They become your obedient servants. If you want something to turn into a mountain, it will do so; or if you wish to create another world, that is also possible. But for this to happen, you don't actually have to reach the final point of realization. You could gain this ability even before that.

"When you are able to concentrate with absolute one-pointedness on certain aspects of the five elements, and are able to retain that one-pointedness, separating the object of your concentration from its inner essence, you will know the essence of everything and be able to control it. You will develop *siddhis* (supernatural powers), by which you can, for example, read people's minds, see and hear things that are happening at a distance, materialize physical objects, know everything about the past and the future, understand any language—including the language of animals, make yourself as light as a feather or as heavy as a mountain, and move through space at any speed or distance.

"In the Indian epics there is a saint called Viswamithra. Before becoming a sage, Viswamithra was a king. He once went on a hunting expedition with a large group of his soldiers. When the hunt was over they were all exhausted and needed to rest. The king remembered that the great sage, Vasistha, had a hermitage in the area, and he led his soldiers there. Vasistha had a divine cow called Nandini, who could fulfill any of the sage's wishes. So when King Viswamithra arrived at the hermitage with his army, Vasistha managed, in no time, to serve them all a grand feast, with the help of the wish-fulfilling cow. Viswamithra was wonderstruck at the power of the cow. He thought to himself that such a precious creature ought to belong to the king of the country, i.e. to himself, and not to a sage who had renounced the world and therefore had no needs. He conveyed his thoughts to the sage, who immediately permitted the king to take the cow. But when the king tried to lead the cow away, the animal protested. She wouldn't move an inch. All the efforts of the king to take her to the palace failed. The king became furious and tried to drag the cow by force with the help of his soldiers. But Nandini responded by creating thousands of fully armed soldiers out of her own body. In the battle that followed, Nandini's soldiers defeated the king's army. Understanding that the cow derived her power from the great sage, the king was enraged and turned to fight the sage, himself. He began showering arrows and other powerful missiles at Vasistha. But the sage was unmoved. With a beaming smile on his face, the sage stood rooted on the ground, holding up his *yogadanda* (the stick of a yogi) in his hand. No thought of enmity, anger, or hatred existed in Vasistha's mind, because he was a true saint, who was beyond the ego and all its negative feelings. All the powerful weapons which the king hurled at him proved to be ineffective before his simple wooden stick. The king was soon disarmed and defeated. He felt deeply humiliated. He was struck by the fact that though he was the most powerful king of his time, his mighty military force and all his weapons were nothing before a great sage like Vasistha, who had immense spiritual powers which he had gained through severe tapas (austerities). The king returned to the palace, boiling with rage. He abdicated from the throne and retired to the forest to do intense tapas. The sole purpose of his tapas was to take revenge on the sage.

"According to the story, Viswamithra did severe tapas and then returned to the world to pour out his vengeance on Vasistha. But each time he tried, his efforts ended in failure. Again and again, he did more tapas, constantly intensifying his practices. He was never discouraged by his failures; he simply continued to do more austerities. Through this he developed such siddhis (yogic powers) that at one point he even managed to create another heaven, a world full of fleeting pleasures, for the sake of challenging Vasistha. Viswamithra performed numerous miracles, but his obsessive anger towards the sage, and his constant miracle making, created countless blocks on his path.

"Eventually, though, his attitude changed, and he finally attained Self-realization. But this could happen only after he had succeeded in eliminating all sense of ego and anger, and had gone beyond the petty feelings of 'I' and 'mine'; when he had given up his vengeful thoughts against the sage, and had learned to love everyone equally; when he stopped using his powers to harm others, and was instead using his powers for the good of everyone, benefiting the entire world.

"There are two aspects to this story. The first shows how genuine the sage Vasistha was. He was a Self-realized master. He had all the divine powers at his disposal, and yet he had no ego. He had no ill feelings towards Viswamithra, who was constantly trying to attack him and insult him. In fact, the epics say that Vasistha, in spite of all the humiliations showered upon him by Viswamithra, praised the latter's greatness and determination on several occasions.

"To begin with, there was a great difference between the two men. While Vasistha maintained a perfect state of mental equilibrium in all circumstances, Viswamithra's hatred was raging within him despite all his achievements. Viswamithra underwent rigorous austerities and attained tremendous spiritual powers. He could perform fantastic miracles; but by doing so, he lost all the powers he had gained through his tapas. He was also constantly in a state of agitation, due to his vengeful thoughts about Vasistha. Because of this, it took a long time for him to reach the state of final emancipation, relative to the intensity of his tapas. Vasistha, on the other hand, was always blissful and serene, and though he also used his divine powers—doing so when and where the need arose—he didn't lose anything by it. Vasistha was purnam (complete). He was one with the Cosmic Power. His spiritual power was inexhaustible, and at the same time he was egoless.

"Nandini, the divine cow, who could fulfill any wish, represents material prosperity (ashtaiswaryas). This means that once you have attained the ultimate state of Self-realization, the whole world with all its wealth will serve you. But because you are beyond all desires, you use that wealth for the benefit and upliftment of society as a whole.

"A person may possess miraculous powers, but as long as he is in the grip of the ego and the feeling of 'I' and 'mine', those powers are useless, because his basic nature remains unchanged, and he himself cannot change or transform anyone. Such a person cannot lead anyone on the path to divinity. A person who misuses his powers can only be destructive and harm society. By using his powers against the laws of nature, he is inevitably paving the way for his own destruction.

"In fact, by performing miracles one upsets the laws of nature. Of course, a Self-realized soul is free to do so, because he is one with the Cosmic Power; but he does so only if it is absolutely necessary, preferring to refrain from it as far as possible.

"While in the highest state of meditation, when their minds were totally attuned to the Universal Energy, the rishis (the ancient seers) saw the mantras, the pure divine vibrations that are the essential principles of the universe. The rishis are the ones who brought these laws into light, for the uplift of society and the benefit of humanity.

"The government, with the help of administrative experts, sets the constitution of a country; and they themselves have to abide by the rules and regulations they have created.

Similarly, in order to set an example, the rishis have to abide by the essential principles which they themselves have revealed, without going beyond and disrupting them.

"The Hindu epics like the *Ramayana,* the *Mahabharata,* and the *Srimad Bhagavatam* contain stories about many kings, demons, demi-gods, and pseudo-masters who have had great powers but could only harm others. Although they were not Self-realized, but were stuck in their egos, they had certain powers. Because of their occult powers they became totally carried away by their egos. They were a curse to humanity. But in the end, they themselves came to grief and perished. So a person may have some supernatural powers without necessarily being Self-realized.

"Spirituality is not meant to feed the ego. On the contrary, spirituality gets rid of the ego; it teaches you to go beyond it. Anyone can develop occult powers by performing certain practices as prescribed by the scriptures. But true spiritual realization is something far beyond such matters. It is a state in which you are completely free from all bondage to the body, mind, and intellect. It is the inner experience of the Supreme Truth. Once that final point has been reached, one cannot harbor any negative feelings, such as anger, hatred, or vengefulness. In that state you dwell in divine love and peace, irrespective of the outer circumstances; and wherever you are, you radiate that same love and peace towards everyone. Your love, compassion, and serenity will transform people. An enlightened being can make the ignorant wise, change mortals into immortals, and man into God. That is the real miracle that happens in the presence of a great soul.

"To go beyond the ego is to become one with the universe. You become as expansive as the universe. You dive deep into its secret mysteries, realizing the ultimate Reality. You become the master of the universe.

"In a Self-realized master's presence, miracles may happen spontaneously; it's simply a natural expression of their being. When a realized soul makes a sankalpa (resolve), it has to manifest. Whatever he thinks inexorably comes into being. If he so wishes, he can transform anything into whatever he wants."

Question: "Amma, you said that the rishis had seen the mantras. What does this mean? Didn't they create the mantras?"

Mother: "No, the mantras have always existed. They are the eternal principles. They are beginningless and without end. They are not created, nor will they ever be destroyed. That is why the *Vedas* are said to be without beginning or end. No one created them. The printed text didn't always exist, but the divine vibrations or mantras which form the *Vedas* have always existed. They were simply revealed to us by the rishis. When it is said that they 'saw', it means that they experienced the *Vedas* in their hearts, when their whole being was at one with the highest point of existence. They experienced what was already there. So they did not create the Vedas (*mantra kartha*);[15] rather, they saw or experienced them (*mantra drishta*).[16]

"When the astronauts landed on the moon, they didn't discover a new moon. They revealed to us what was already there. They saw and experienced the moon, and then, through pictures and words, they transferred what they saw to us. It is the same with the mantras."

The brahmacharis began singing *Radhe Govinda Gopi Gopala*, and Amma took the lead.

O Radha
Lord of the Cows
Milkmaid
Cowherd Boy
Lord of the Cows
Cowherd Boy
Salutations to the Son of Nanda
O Radha
Lord of the Cows
Milkmaid
Cowherd Boy

Mira Bai's Lord
Flute playing Cowherd Boy
Who lifted up the Govardhana Hill
Boy Gopala
O Radha

---

[15] Mantra kartha = creator or author of a mantra. The Sanskrit word 'kartha' means 'the doer' or 'the author.' The rishis are not mantra kartha.

[16] Mantra drishta = perceiver of a mantra. The word 'drishta' means 'seer' or 'perceiver.' It is derived from the root, 'drish,' meaning 'to see.' It implies that the mantras have always existed on the subtle plane; and the rishis discovered them, that is, they perceived them. So the rishis are mantra drishta.

Lord of the Cows
Milkmaid
Cowherd Boy

Are miracles relevant?

Question: "Amma, should miracles be encouraged, or are they obstacles on the spiritual path?"

Mother: "For an ordinary person miracles can be of some help to instill faith in a supreme power. But any faith that is rooted only in miracles can also easily be lost when the miracles are not forthcoming. What if God, or a great soul who is one with God, who is omnipresent, omnipotent, and omniscient, decides not to perform an expected miracle? It can happen because such a soul doesn't owe anything to anyone, and has nothing to gain or lose by performing miracles. It makes no difference to God or to a great saint whether or not people believe in Him. He doesn't need our faith or our service. It is we who need His grace. But His grace can only be obtained through faith.

"A perfect master doesn't need anything from us, for he is complete as he is. It is we who need his grace to purify and uplift us. Our faith shouldn't depend merely on miracles. Faith for its own sake, and love for love's own sake, is the healthiest and wisest approach.

"Our faith should be rooted in both the heart and the intellect. For a true sadhak, both devotion and intellectual knowledge are necessary—unless, of course, we posses the same intense love, total faith and self-surrender that the gopis of Vrindavan had. Though their love was a type of blind love in the beginning, it gradually evolved into *tatwattile bhakti* (devotion rooted in the essential principles of spirituality), which is bhakti grounded in jnana.

"We should feel both love and respect for God or a perfect spiritual master—love of the heart and the respect that arises from an understanding of the master's all-pervasive, omnipotent, and omniscient nature. Only then will we receive the full benefit of his presence. It is the blend of love and knowledge that helps us to fully experience the grace of God or a true master in our lives. But that inner experience of God's blissful presence cannot be experienced if one is too obsessed with miracles.

"Miracles do have a place, but we shouldn't give them too much importance. People have a tendency to get too attached to such things. When this happens, people lose their perspective, and the miracles themselves become the sole point of focus.

"People who have too many desires tend to give too much importance to miracles. Their faith is shallow. Too many miracles will only serve to create even more desires in the minds of such people, and their desires will only lead to sorrow and suffering.

"True spirituality is to go beyond all desires, to go beyond the mind and its thoughts. This is what a true aspirant longs for. A genuine seeker is not satisfied with anything less than the state beyond the mind, and miracles cannot help you reach that state. If anything, they will only be a hindrance, because a person who is attached to miracles is stuck at the level of the mind and its demands to be stimulated—and that, of course, is not the ultimate state.

"In the spiritual pursuit, while the aspirant is advancing in his sadhana, he may develop the power to perform miracles. Whereas a less sincere seeker may get trapped in the power of such abilities, the true seeker, who genuinely wishes to realize the ultimate Truth, will ignore such things and transcend them.

"People consider materializing objects and curing diseases to be the only kinds of miracles. Such things are, of course, miracles of a sort; but the greatest miracle is the inner transformation that happens to a person. People don't consider that the real miracle consists of the opening of one's heart into the one Supreme Truth. If they were to just open up their hearts, they would experience the real miracle—they would realize that God's grace is always present—nay, that they themselves are God—and that miracles are happening at every moment.

"Everything in nature is a wonderful miracle. Isn't a little bird flying through the vast sky a miracle? Isn't a tiny fish swimming in the depths of the ocean a miracle? Unfortunately, people think that only if a fish flies through the sky can it be called a miracle!

"True spirituality and true religion has little to do with performing miracles, nor is the amount of miracles a person performs a criterion by which to measure his divinity. True spirituality is to be found in the immeasurable love and inner peace that the master transmits to others. True spirituality is expressed as pure love and perfect equanimity. Only through love can a real transformation be brought about. A harmonious blend of selfless love and pure knowledge will remove all misconceptions about spirituality."

In Mother's lap

One by one, the people were called by Mother and came up to Her. A man came up and, as he lay his head in Mother's lap, Mother began to sing *Sri Krishna Sharanam Mama.*

Sri Krishna is my Refuge
Sri Hari is my Refuge

Prostrations to Sri Krishna
Whose nature is Being-Awareness-Bliss
Who is the Cause of the creation, preservation, and
dissolution of the universe
Destroyer of the three types of suffering

I know no Reality other than Sri Krishna
Who holds the flute in His hands
Who is beautiful like a fresh rain cloud
Who wears yellow robes
Whose lips are red like an aruna bimba fruit
Whose face is charming like the full moon
And whose eyes are slanted like lotus petals.

Sri Krishna, how sweet is Your Name!
O Son of Nanda, how sweet is Your Name!
O Moon of Vrindavan
Sri Krishna is the Name that is dear to You
All these Names are dear to You

Victory to Radha Govinda!
Victory to Radha Gopal
Govinda, Govinda, Goparipal (Protector of the cows)!

Some say You are the son of Vasudeva
Others call you the son of Nanda

On the banks of the Yamuna river
The Child Krishna plays the flute so sweetly
Sri Krishna is a Name that is dear to You
The One Who Loves to Dance is a name that is dear to You
Protector of the Sages is a name that is dear to You

Mother suddenly went into a state of rapture, and in that state She continued to sing for at least ten minutes. She kept repeating the refrain of the song: "Sri Krishna Sharanam Mama, Sri Hari Sharanam Mama…." At the end of the song, She was in a deeply absorbed mood, which lasted for another ten minutes.

When Mother finally opened Her eyes, the man who had been receiving darshan all this time was still kneeling in front of Her, resting in Her lap. Mother gently tapped him on the shoulder as a sign for him to get up. He didn't move. Again Mother tapped his shoulder, but there was no response. Mother said to him, "Son, get up." But nothing happened. Mother used a little more force by lifting his head slightly and calling louder, "Son!" This time he jumped up with a start. He looked as if he had just emerged from another world. He rubbed his eyes and looked around confused. Everyone thought they understood what had happened to him, that he had fallen fast asleep in Mother's lap, and they laughed heartily. Mother also burst out laughing; but a moment later, when She saw the innocent, helpless expression on his face, She took his hand and made him sit down on the floor next to Her chair, and She affectionately put his head back on Her lap. As the laughter slowly subsided, the man sat up and Mother continued giving darshan.

While the next person was receiving Mother's darshan, She turned to Amritatma and said, "He was in bliss!"

Only a few people came to know what had really happened. As the man was resting in Her lap, Mother had begun singing. After a minute or two, he suddenly had the experience that Mother's lap was growing; and as Her lap continued to expand, the depth and intensity of the bliss he was experiencing also increased. At last he felt that he was swimming in an ocean of bliss. He remained in a state of merging until Mother finally brought him out of it.

❧❧

Austria

Put others before yourself

From Switzerland Mother took a train to Austria, where two programs had been arranged by a woman called Christine Essen—one program in Graz and the other, a residential program, in St. Polten, a small town between Vienna and Linz. Austria was to be the last stop on the tour.

While traveling on the train the brahmacharis had an opportunity to spend some time alone with Mother. At one point, Mother said to them: "People ask why they are being put through such severe tests in life; why they, of all people, have to suffer. 'Why me?' is the question. They don't seem to care if it happens to anyone else. Their attitude is, 'Let someone else suffer, as long as it isn't me.' Let us change that attitude and, instead, sincerely wish that no one in the world should have to suffer. Let us not think, 'Why me?' but rather, 'Why should anyone have to suffer?' Let us learn to put others before ourselves. Amma has heard the following story:

"A little boy was staring in wonder at a beautiful, newly-built mansion. As he stood in front of the house, a young man came out of the gate. The boy asked him, 'Who does that beautiful house belong to?' 'It's mine,' said the man. 'I have a brother who happens to be very rich. He built it for me.' Hearing this the boy exclaimed, 'Oh, if only...' and he sighed deeply. The man could easily guess what the boy was about to say next—that if only he had a brother like that.... But when the boy continued to speak, the man was surprised by what he said. 'Oh,' said the boy, 'if only I was a brother like that!'

"Children, it is this sort of attitude that brings joy to our lives. Why should anyone have to suffer in this world? If you are good-hearted enough to put others before yourself, you will experience peace and happiness. But for this to happen, you have to move away from selfishness and journey along the path to selflessness.

"People have a tendency to want more and more and more. They are never satisfied with what they have. Instead, we should learn to give and to share. We should never be mere takers.

"We should share whatever we have with others; and we should try to contribute to the welfare of society in some way. It is through giving that we progress on the spiritual path. If we hoard our wealth, our spiritual development will be stunted, and slowly our lives will wither away. The blood that is pumped by the heart is circulated and distributed evenly throughout the whole body. What would happen if our circulation were to stop? We would collapse and die. Likewise, whatever we have should be circulated and shared. We shouldn't hoard our wealth because then society becomes stagnant, and cannot grow as a whole.

"It is through selfless sharing that the flower of life becomes beautiful and fragrant."

In Mother's own life there are countless examples that clearly show Her selfless love and compassion.

In the early days, the financial position of the ashram was very poor. Sometimes the residents didn't have enough to eat. They had only one set of clothes each, and whenever they had to attend Mother's programs outside the ashram, they would share the few good clothes that were available. Also, Mother was very particular that the visitors who came to the ashram should be given food. Only after all the guests had been served were the residents allowed to eat. Because they never knew how many people would arrive on any given day, and because there was hardly any money available, there was often no food left for the residents. On those occasions, Mother would go to the neighboring houses and beg for food.

One day a woman from the neighborhood came to Mother and told Her that the marriage of her daughter had been arranged. Because the woman was very poor, she asked Mother to help her. Even though the ashram was struggling financially, Mother assured her that She would help. She called one of the brahmacharis and asked him to fetch a box from Her room. When the box was brought to Mother, She opened it and took out a brand new, gold necklace, which someone had recently given Her.

Br. Ramakrishnan (Swami Ramakrishnananda), who was sitting next to Mother, was wondering what Mother was about to do. Without the slightest hesitation, Mother handed the necklace to the destitute woman. Ramakrishnan was shocked at this because the ashramites themselves were so poor. At the time, he was working in a bank, and he knew the value of that necklace.

By the time the woman had left, he was so agitated that he could no longer control himself. He blurted out, "Amma, how could you do such a thing! Do you know how valuable that necklace is? I could have taken it to the bank for you and received a lot of money for it. You shouldn't have done that!"

Mother replied, "Is that so? Why didn't you tell me earlier? Hurry up! Go and call her back immediately!"

Ramakrishnan was very pleased with Mother's response. He felt proud of himself for having been able to correct Mother's mistake. He ran to the woman and brought her back to Mother. The woman looked bewildered. Mother pointed at Ramakrishnan and said to her, "This brahmachari says that the necklace Amma gave you is worth a great deal of money."

Ramakrishnan was so impatient, he was about to interrupt and tell the woman to give it back, when Mother turned to him and told him to keep quiet. She continued, "Because the necklace is so valuable, whatever you do, don't pawn it or sell it for a cheaper price than it is worth. Make sure you get a good price for it."

Ramakrishnan suddenly felt deeply ashamed of himself, for not having understood the extent of Mother's compassion.

The train moved along, making the sound, "chuck, chuck, chuck...." Outside the train window the sun was beginning to set. Mother asked the brahmacharis to sing the usual evening bhajans. Mother was very particular that the brahmacharis should stick to their daily spiritual practices, no matter where they were. She often told them that a sadhak should not be enslaved by circumstances, but should be the master of all situations.

Br. Srikumar took the harmonium out of its carrying case and began to play. During the next hour and a half they sang several songs. One of them was called *Orunalil Varumo*.

O Mother of unearthly bliss,
Won't You come one day to the shrine of my heart
With Your eternally shining lamp?
It is for this reason alone
That this supplicant is wandering about.

O Devi,
Won't You bless me?
With a melting heart
I have searched for the Divine Mother everywhere.
O Mother, bestow Your Grace upon me;
Caress me with Your soft hands.

O Mother, give me shelter;
I am collapsing with exhaustion.
I know it is true that You dwell in me
But when will the day of realization come?

During the bhajans, Mother intermittently joined in the singing, but most of the time She sat quietly looking out through the window.

One evening in Vienna there was no program. Mother, along with the group who was traveling with Her, went out for a stroll. They walked along a country road for about half an hour, until Mother sat down beside a beautiful wooded area, with Her face towards the setting sun. It was only seven degrees Celsius. The few people who passed them on the road were wearing several layers of warm clothes. Mother was just wearing Her white sari. Someone covered Her with a woolen shawl. The brahmacharis were wearing nothing but their dhotis and cotton shirts, and they were freezing. Seeing the brahmacharis huddled together, shivering with cold, Mother removed Her shawl and lovingly wrapped it around them. But as Mother would then have nothing to protect Her from the cold, the brahmacharis politely refused, saying, "No Amma, you should wear it." But Mother refused to put it on again. "No problem!" She said, insisting that they use it. The shawl which Mother so lovingly insisted that they wear was so precious to them that they all wanted to be covered by it; so they all huddled close together.

Brahmashakti

Still sitting huddled under the shawl, Br. Ramakrishna asked Mother a question:

"Amma, it is said that the divine sankalpa of the Paramatman (the Supreme Self) is everywhere. What does this mean? Could you please explain?"

Mother: "The Paramatman's sankalpa or *Brahmashakti* (the power of Brahman) underlies everything in the universe. Look at this amazing cosmos and the harmonious way in which our planet and all other planets function. Without a cosmic intelligence, a universal power that controls everything, how could such perfect order and beauty exist? Can we call it accidental? No, because nothing is accidental. Whenever there is something the human intellect cannot explain, we dismiss it and call it accidental. But that is the language of intellectual reasoning. A person who functions more from the heart doesn't think of anything as mere chance. He calls it God's power, God's *leela* (play), or sankalpa.

"Amma is not trying to deny the value of science and its contributions. Science has a certain dharma (duty) to fulfill. Let science follow its dharma; but let us remember that, as human beings who are trying to live our lives attuned to God, we have a dharma of our own which we should adhere to. We should live our lives accordingly, listening to the call of our inner conscience.

"The ego or the intellect cannot comprehend or even begin to perceive the great sankalpa that is the power behind the universe. Science is still searching for that cosmic intelligence. But unless the scientists create a balance between science and spirituality, they will not find the life-giving Principle which is beyond the intellect. The inner world, which is normally given no importance, needs to be explored if they wish to understand what lies behind the outer world.

"A beautiful melody emerging from a flute is neither to be found in the flute nor in the player's fingertips. You could say it comes from the composer's heart. But if you were to open up his heart and take a look, you wouldn't find it there either. What, then, is the original source of the music? The source is beyond; it emerges out of Brahmashakti, the Paramatman. But the ego cannot recognize this power. Only if you learn to function from the heart can you really see and feel this divine power in your life.

"God's sankalpa is behind everything—behind the blossoming of a flower, the chirping of a bird, the movement of the wind, and the flames of a fire. It is the power by which everything grows;

it is the power that sustains everything. That divine sankalpa is the underlying cause of the birth, growth, and death of all living beings. It is the cause of the entire creation. It is the Paramatman's shakti that sustains the world. Without it, the world would cease to exist."

Mother turned to Amritatma and asked him to sing *Kodanukodi*.

O Eternal Truth,
For millions of years
Mankind has been searching for You.

The ancient sages renounced everything,
And for the purpose of making the Self flow,
Through meditation,
Into Your Divine Stream,
They performed endless years of austerities.

Your infinitesimal Flame,
Inaccessible to all,
Shines like the blaze of the sun;
It stands perfectly still, without a flutter
In the fierce wind of the cyclone.

The flowers and creepers,
The shrine rooms and temples,
With their newly installed sacred pillars,
Have been waiting for You for eons
And yet You remain unreachable.

After the song Mother continued speaking:

"Do you know the story of when Brahman appeared among the *devas* (celestial beings)? Brahmashakti (the power of the Absolute Reality) won a victory for the devas. But the devas gave all the credit to themselves. They chose to believe they had won solely because of their own greatness. Drunk with their egos, the devas forgot about Brahman, as they rejoiced and celebrated their victory on a grand scale. When Brahman came to know of this, He appeared before them in the form of a *yaksha*, an adorable spirit. Being totally carried away by their egos, the devas failed to recognize Him, who was the very cause and power behind the victory they were celebrating. When the yaksha appeared, Indra, the chief of the devas, sent the god of fire, [17] to find out who the spirit was. When the fire god approached the yaksha, the spirit asked him who he was and what his powers were.

"With great pride, the god replied, 'I am the deity presiding over fire. There is nothing in the world I cannot burn.'

"Brahman, in the form of the yaksha, placed a single straw in front of the god and asked him to burn it.

"The god tried with all his might, but no matter how hard he tried, he wasn't able to leave the slightest mark on the straw. He withdrew and reported to Indra that he didn't know who the yaksha was. He didn't mention a word about his own defeat, because the ego never accepts defeat.

"While the ego places great importance on its own achievements, it refuses to admit any of its failures. This is human nature. People say, 'I have achieved this and that,' but they rarely say, 'I was defeated,' or, 'I have failed in such and such an area of my life.' Because of their lack of humility, they get carried away by their egos, and become drunk with the idea of power and wealth. They fail to see the Universal Power, God's sankalpa, in their day-to-day achievements, and also in their failures. If everything is pervaded with God's sankalpa, our failures are also His sankalpa. But people do not see His sankalpa anywhere. They believe that whenever they succeed, it is due to their own power and greatness.

---

[17] The Hindus consider all the natural forces to be deities, and worship them as different aspects of the Supreme.

On the other hand, when they fail, they refuse to admit they had anything to do with it. Instead they blame their failures on others or on different situations.

"When Brahman appeared, the fire god wasn't able to recognize him. This is a typical example of how the ego works. The ego is proud of its own apparent power and cleverness, while it ignores the Universal Power. Even when that Supreme Power appears in front of us in manifold forms, we fail to recognize it. How could fire burn if the Paramatman's Shakti, the Supreme Shakti—the power behind all fire—was not present? This is why the god of fire became powerless and was defeated.

"Indra then commanded Vayu, the god of air, to approach the spirit. Vayu went up to the spirit, introduced himself, and boasted that there was nothing on earth that he couldn't blow away. The yaksha placed the straw in front of Vayu and said, 'You claim to be so powerful. Then blow this away!' Vayu huffed and puffed at the straw with all his might, but the straw wouldn't budge.

"The ego likes to make a great huff about its own importance. But how could the ego function without the life force behind it? Agni (fire) and Vayu (air) are just minuscule points of the Universal Energy. If that energy is withdrawn, they lose all their power. In other words, it is the Cosmic Energy that functions through fire and air, without which they wouldn't exist.

"Vayu also refused to admit his defeat. All he said to Indra was that he didn't know who the yaksha was either.

"People think that their sense organs (devas) are very important and give them great credit, but when they find themselves in situations in which they are helpless or defeated, they turn to the mind or the intellect for help, which is higher and subtler than the senses.

"Now all the devas (gods) came together and asked Indra (the mind and intellect, that is, the chief of the senses) to find out who the yaksha was. But when Indra, who by now was a bit humbled, approached the yaksha, the spirit disappeared and in its place he beheld the great, effulgent Goddess Uma. Indra asked Her, 'Who was that adorable spirit (yaksha)?'

"Uma, the Universal Mother, said to Indra, 'That was Brahmashakti, who won your victory for you. What you believed to be your victory, was actually *His* victory. It was only through Him that any of your glory was achieved.'

"So, whatever you achieve in life, it is not your but Brahman's achievement. The Paramatman's sankalpa lies behind each one of your victories and failures. Learn to recognize it; for in that understanding lies true success in life.

"In your quest to understand the Cosmic Energy, the Supreme Consciousness, with your mind, senses, and intellect, you will always be confronted with defeat, though you may not accept it as such; because the Atman or Brahman is beyond the intellect; it is subtler than the senses, mind, and intellect—subtler than the subtlest. Out of your utter inability to understand, a strong urge will be created within you to know what that great power is. In your state of helplessness, you finally give up, and this leads to the surrender of your mind. It is this surrender that brings your 'beloved', the master, to you. The master will help you and guide you to the real source of existence. In reality, the master himself is Brahmashakti. The form exists as long as you are identified with the body and mind. Once you have transcended the body and mind, you will experience the infinite, formless aspect of the master.

"The *Vedas* say that the universe emerged out of the Paramatman's breath. The meaning of this is that it is the Supreme Life Principle or Vital Energy that functions throughout creation. When that Principle withdraws by itself, everything stops. The very purpose of life is to recognize the Divine Principle (sankalpa) in all our thoughts and actions, and in every aspect of life."

Mother turned to Br. Srikumar and said, "Bring the harmonium." The harmonium was back at the house where they were staying, but, as he had anticipated that something like this might happen, he was carrying a small keyboard. He showed this to Mother, and She accepted it. Then, to Srikumar's accompaniment, Mother sang a bhajan called *Sokamitentinu Sandhye.*

> *O twilight, why are you so sad?*
> *Are you also wandering*
> *On the shores of your memories?*
> *O dusk, bathed in shades of red,*
> *Does the fire of sorrow burn within you?*
>
> *O twilight, do you have a Mother like mine?*
> *Have you seen my Mother?*
> *She radiates beauty and cool purity*
> *Like the full moon.*
>
> *O dusk, if you should see Her,*
> *Please convey the message of this helpless child,*
> *Who cannot speak.*
> *I am weighted down with infinite sorrow,*
> *Caused by the pain of separation.*
>
> *O twilight, please offer these flower petals at Her feet*
> *And convey my words.*
> *When you return, I shall tell you*
> *My sweet stories of a bygone spring.*

Mother continued to sing two more songs. While everyone was shivering in the cold, Mother seemed totally unaffected. It was as if the cold air was too timid to come close to Her. A little later Mother stood up and they all walked back along the road.

It has happened many times that Mother has asked for a cardigan or a pair of woolen socks, or even a heater, when it is very hot. But when it's cold, it doesn't seem to affect Her at all. It is impossible to understand Mother. Her ways are often incomprehensible. Even Her body is subject to entirely different laws than those of any ordinary person.

Mother's first world tour was coming to an end.
She had blessed the land of many countries with the touch of Her sacred feet; and who knows what effect that was to have on those countries in years to come? Mother works on different levels, most of them so subtle that we cannot even begin to perceive them. We can only see the tip of the iceberg of what Mother is doing on this planet.

The 1987 world tour was the beginning of a spiritual conquest by that great Conqueror of hearts. In the years to come, Mother was to return to the West, again and again, bringing countless people to the spiritual path, and gathering those already on the path under Her wing of Grace.

Mother had spent just a few days in each place, passing through like a sweet whirlwind of Supreme Love, leaving in Her wake countless hearts awakened with a new, strange longing for a spiritual life, a yearning to know God, which could not be extinguished. No one who had met Mother would ever be able to forget Her; and those whose hearts She had captured in Her divine net found that they were beginning to change; that their hard edges were softening, and that, as a result of the immeasurable love that Mother had given them, they themselves were beginning to feel a compassion towards others that they had never known.

In countless people, Mother had transformed pain into joy, despair into hope, sickness into health, fear into peace, lack of meaning into renewed faith, and indifference into love and compassion. People's hearts had been touched by Her Grace.

On their way back to India, Mother and the group had a stopover in the Maldives. Near the airport they got into a small motor boat and were driven out to one of the islands where they were to stay overnight.

When they arrived on the island, the group enjoyed a very special day, an opportunity to be alone with Mother. Mother spent most of the day outside. They all sat together on the beach, meditating and singing bhajans. Nealu put on a diving mask and dived into the shallows. When he came back up to the surface, he excitedly told Mother that he had seen a variety of multicolored fish. Mother got up, saying, "That old man always wants to amuse Amma and make Her happy! He finds all sorts of different methods to accomplish this." Mother looked down into the clear water. She spotted several fish and started shouting and jumping up and down like an excited child. Suddenly, Mother stopped, and like a persistent child demanded to be given something to feed the fish. Nealu happened to have some nuts and Indian mixture with him, which he gave Mother. With Her face bathing in bliss, She fed the fish. As She stood gazing down at the brightly colored creatures, She went into a state of rapture. She sat down at the edge of the water and became immersed in samadhi. Everyone sat down close to Her. When Mother finally emerged from that state, She softly sang the Sanskrit hymn, *Vidamsam vibhum.*

> *Again and again, I salute Parabrahman, the Absolute Reality, which is one without a second, permeates everything in the universe, and is pure and totally auspicious; yet, which, at the same time, is beyond all attributes—the Unmanifest, the fourth and highest point of consciousness.*

It started to drizzle. Mother didn't move, but continued to sit at the edge of the water.

The awakening of the inner child

Br. Nealu took the opportunity to ask Mother a question.

"Is it the duty of a Self-realized being to lead others towards the goal? Isn't that the obligation of such a soul?"

Mother: "Obligations exist only on the mental and physical plane. Once you transcend the mind and realize you are not an isolated entity, not just a part, but the whole—the Cosmic Energy itself—then there is nobody, or no body, to feel obliged. A satguru, who is one with existence, doesn't owe anything to anyone, he has no obligations whatsoever. His life is perfect and complete as it is. He simply exists, as a great, divine Presence. Does infinite space owe anything to anyone? Does the sun, the wind, or the oceans owe anything to anyone? They simply exist; and we benefit by their existence. What do the great masters need from us? It is we who owe everything to them.

"We have nothing to offer those who are willing to sacrifice their lives for the sake of the world. It is only because of their grace that we may receive the unique gift of God-realization. Isn't such an immeasurable gift far more than anyone could ask for? We can only bow down to them with great humility, and be immensely grateful to them for coming down to us and helping us evolve to the plane of supreme bliss, where they themselves dwell eternally.

"Guiding a disciple to the supreme goal of God-realization is like giving birth to a baby and carefully raising it; that is the only way to describe it. Staying in the presence of a satguru is like being born again; it's like a second birth.

"Until this point, you have developed only externally, only the body and intellect have grown. But once you come to a satguru, an inner development takes place and you grow into the experience of the soul (Atman). Externally, you may be grown-up; but internally, the master teaches you to go back to the state of a child, to the state of childlike innocence. The master's whole purpose is to awaken the slumbering child within you.

"When a mother breast-feeds her baby and gives it other nourishing food, and when she provides the child with all the love and warmth it needs, she is creating the necessary conditions that will enable the child to grow and develop properly. Just as a mother creates the most favorable conditions for the healthy development of her child, a true master creates a conducive atmosphere for the innate innocence to awaken and develop in the disciple. The satguru's presence, look, and touch is the food that is needed for the sleeping inner child of the disciple to awaken and to develop.

"Think of the tremendous amount of love and care your mother bestowed on you, the patience she had in helping you to grow up and become a young man or woman. Most of us owe much to our mothers for our mental and physical development. She took care of us without expecting anything in return. She did it simply out of the immeasurable love she felt for her child.

"If you can imagine this picture of a mother, selflessly nourishing and nurturing her children, you will get an idea of how a spiritual master brings up his disciples; how the master helps the disciples to grow out of their ego and become as expansive as the universe. This simile of a mother raising her child is only an example to help you understand the great task of the master in transforming the disciple, of turning the disciple into a pure vessel of supreme power. A true master must be as patient as the earth to do this. You could say that by performing this miracle, he is more loving and compassionate than God Himself. By this, Amma means that we do not know anything about God, except the extremely vague concepts we have received through stories and the scriptures. It is only through the immense compassion of a satguru that we are able to experience God in a tangible way. It is in the satguru's presence that we come to know that God really exists.

"When the disciple approaches the master, he is raw, rusty, and primitive. The master, the infinitely loving, divine alchemist, transforms the disciple into pure 'gold.' The master doesn't have to do this. He has a choice and could simply dissolve into the Totality without ever uttering a word. But, instead, he chooses to become an offering to the world. He sacrifices himself out of sheer compassion for those who are groping in the dark."

Bri. Gayatri was trying to hold an umbrella over Mother. But Mother refused to accept it. "No," She said, "as long as Amma's children are in the rain, She doesn't want an umbrella." But soon it began to rain so heavily that Mother and the others went back to their rooms.

A wonderful cosmic play

That night, when the rain had stopped, Mother and the entire group walked out to the end of a pier and sat down together in a thatched gazebo. Mother sang several hymns and the group responded in the traditional way.

A full moon illumined the earth and sea. The waves reverberated with their eternal chanting of "Aum." Mother's pure voice and the power and beauty of Her presence uplifted the souls of Her children, and lent the atmosphere a unique spiritual glow.

She sang, *Samsara Dukha Samanam...*

> *O Mother of the world,*
> *Dispeller of the sorrows of transmigration,*
> *The shelter of Your blessed Hand*
> *Is our only refuge.*

You are the refuge of lost and blind souls;
By remembering Your Lotus Feet
We are protected from danger.

For the deluded ones,
Who are immersed in impenetrable darkness,
Meditation on Your name and form
Is the only escape from their wretched state.

Let Your beautiful, radiant eyes
Cast a glance at my mind;
O Mother, Your Grace is the only way
To reach Your Lotus Feet.

The following day they took the little motor boat back to the main island. It was a windy day. As the boat headed out towards the sea, a storm suddenly blew up and the sea became extremely rough. The little boat was being tossed up and down like a toy among the waves. At times the waves were so gigantic it seemed they would crash into the boat. The brahmacharis, Gayatri, Saumya, and the others were terrified. They were cowering in the boat, trembling with fear. Several waves came very close to breaking into the boat. They were sure the little vessel would fill with water at any moment and they would sink.

Suddenly, through the wind and the roar of the waves they heard someone laughing. They looked up and realized it was Mother. Mother was thoroughly enjoying Herself. She kept laughing and Her face had the expression of a delighted child. At that moment, they understood that Mother is completely fearless, and that for Her, every situation in life is just part of a wonderful cosmic play.

Listening to Mother's blissful laughter they calmed down and were no longer afraid. For what need is there to fear when the Mother of the Universe Herself is sitting by your side, as you cross the ocean of life?

OM NAMAH SHIVAYA

Glossary

Advaita: A school of philosophy that declares that Non-duality is the highest Truth, that all that exists is that One Truth in so many forms.

Anugraha: Divine Grace.

Arati: Vespers, waving the burning camphor, which leaves no residue, with ringing of bells at the end of worship, representing the complete offering of the ego to God.

Arjuna: Cousin and close friend of Lord Krishna, to whom the Lord told the Bhagavad Gita.

Ashtaiswaryas: The eight Treasures.

Atma Jnana: Self-knowledge

Atman: The true Self. We are the eternal, pure, unblemishable Self.

Avatar: An incarnation of God.

Bhagavad Gita: The Song of God, a discourse between Lord Krishna and His devotee Arjuna, delivered at the start of the Mahabharata War about five thousand years ago.

Bhajan: Devotional singing.

Brahmachari: Celibate student.

Brahman: The Absolute Reality.

Darshan: Audience of a holy person or deity.

Deva: A god or being of light.

Devi Bhava: Amma's mood as the Divine Mother.

Devi Mahatmyam: An ancient text in praise of the Divine Mother

Dharma: Righteousness, in accordance with Divine Harmony.

Durga Suktam: A portion of the Vedas praising the Divine Mother Durga.

Ganesh: Lord of obstacles, son of Lord Shiva, God with an elephant face.

Grihastashrami: A person leading a married life while practicing sadhana at the same time.

Guru: Teacher or spiritual master.

Gurukula: A Guru's ashram where students gain a foundation in spiritual and worldly knowledge through study and service.

Japa: Repetition of a mantra.

Jivanmukti: Liberation while living in the human body.

Jivatman: The individual soul.

Jnana Yoga: The Path of Knowledge.

Jnani: A Knower of Reality, a Self-realized soul.

Karma Kanda: The portion of the Vedas that prescribes various duties to be performed during one's life.

Karma Yoga: The path of action.

Katha: A story.

Kauravas: Cousins of Lord Krishna who fought in the Mahabharata War against the Pandavas.

Krishna: An incarnation of Lord Vishnu.

Leela: A divine play or show, appearance.

Mahabharata: An epic of ancient India, written by the sage Vyasa, about the family fight between the Pandavas and the Kauravas, both cousins of Lord Krishna, which culminated in a catastrophic war.

Mahatma: Great Soul or Sage.

Mantra Shakti: The power of a mantra to bestow a particular result.

Maya: Illusion.

Moksha: Release from the cycle of birth and death.

Mudra: Hand pose indicative of mystic truths.

Ojas: Spiritual energy derived from spiritual practices and celibacy.

Pada puja: Worship of the feet of God or a saint.

Pandavas: Cousins of Lord Krishna who fought in the Mahabharata War against the Kauravas.

Paramatman: The Supreme Soul or God.

Prasad: Consecrated offerings distributed at the end of worship.

Purnam: Full or perfect.

Rajasuya Yagna: A Vedic sacrifice performed by kings.

Ramayana: The epic story of Lord Rama, written by the sage
Valmiki.

Ravana: A demonic king in the story of the Ramayana.

Rishis: The seers of ancient times to whom Divine Knowledge
was revealed and who transmitted it to their disciples.

Sadhak: A spiritual aspirant.

Sadhana: Spiritual practice.

Samadhi: Absorption of the mind into Reality or Truth.

Samsara: The illusory cycle of birth, death and rebirth.

Sankalpa: A resolve.

Sannyasin: One who has taken formal vows of renunciation.

Sari: The common dress worn by Indian women.

Satchitananda: The Supreme Reality as absolute Existence, Awareness, Bliss.

Satguru: Self-realized master.

Shraddha: Care, attentiveness, faith.

Siddhi: Psychic power.

Sita: Consort of Lord Rama.

Slokas: Verses.

Sri Rama: An incarnation of Lord Vishnu.

Tantra: A school of philosophy that teaches that everything in
creation is a manifestation of the Supreme Reality.

Tapas: Austerity, hardship undergone for the sake of self-purifi-
cation.

Tattvatile Bhakti: Devotion based on spiritual knowledge and
principles.

Upanishads: Concluding portion of the Vedas containing teachings on the science of Self-knowledge.

Vasanas: Residual impressions of objects and actions experienced; habits.

Vedanta: The "end of the Vedas", the Upanishads which delineate the Path of Knowledge.

Vedas: The authoritative scriptures of the Hindus, lit. "Knowledge."

Veena: A stringed instrument of ancient India.

Videhamukti: Liberation after physical death.

Yaga or Yagnya: Vedic sacrifice or ritual.

Yaksha: A powerful being that exists in the subtle planes of the universe.

Yoga danda: A staff on which a yogi may support himself during prolonged meditation.

Yoga Sutras: A philosophical work by the sage Patanjali which delineates the path of Raja Yoga or the yogic "path of eight limbs" (ashtanga).

Yogi: A person engaged in spiritual practice in order to attain union with the Divine Source or God.

Yuga: An age or era.